THE JOHNSON FAMILY SINGERS

THE JOHNSON FAMILY SINGERS

We Sang for Our Supper

Kenneth M. Johnson

Introduction by Charles Wolfe

University Press of Mississippi   Jackson

Library of Congress Cataloging-in-Publication Data

Johnson, Kenneth M., 1928–

    The Johnson family singers : we sang for our supper /
Kenneth M. Johnson.

      p. cm.

    Includes index.

    Discography: p.

    ISBN 1-57806-003-6 (cloth : alk. paper)—
ISBN 1-57806-004-4 (pbk. : alk. paper)

    1. Johnson Family Singers.   2. Gospel musicians—United
States—Biography.

ML421.J64J6   1997

782.25'4'0922—dc21

    [B]   97-14034
                                               CIP
                                           MN

British Library Cataloging-in-Publication data available

To the memory of our parents:

"Pa" Johnson, originator, and

"Ma" Johnson, producer,

of the Johnson Family Singers

CONTENTS

PREFACE

After listening to the cassette tape of an old Johnson Family radio show in the summer of 1979, a friend wrote: "I have listened to it with great pleasure, and I will be sharing it with others who I am sure will also enjoy it. Thanks very much for sending it and for your contribution to our American heritage." These words were not only flattering but also motivational. I took another look at the phonograph records the family had made and jotted down a few notes here and there. Before I knew it, the narrative of my family's experiences had begun to take shape.

So, I set about to write the story of what radio station WBT in Charlotte, North Carolina, had called "one of America's foremost singing families"—a family whose career peaked in popularity during the golden days of radio. This account puts together the life and times of the Johnson Family Singers and shows how on several occasions in dire circumstances we not only "sang for our supper" but found great pleasure and excitement in doing it.

Here is a tale of a persevering father, a devoted mother, and some talented children who achieved stardom despite modest beginnings. References to persons living or dead are intentional, making this story a saga of real people and of events that helped my family reach a position of national prominence at the zenith of radio's popularity, just before the proliferation of television sets in living rooms across the nation.

For thirteen years, from 1938 to 1951, even though we sometimes literally sang for our supper, we didn't always eat! Even so, we managed to perform on WBT, "the radio voice of the South," as well as on numerous CBS network programs. One of our Columbia records, "The Old Rugged Cross" (ZSP 7175), was included in that company's Hall of Fame Series. Another song, "The Death of Ellenton"

(Columbia 20895), was included in the Library of Congress *Folk Music in America* collection (*Volume 12: Songs of Local History and Events*, LCM 2095).

Mother's death in the spring of 1979 reminded me of the mortality of the people who could help me to compile and write the family story. I made a special trip that winter to see my father, whom I interviewed about his early life and the beginnings of the Johnson Family Singers. I discussed the project extensively with my sister and brothers, revisited former neighbors and friends, and talked to our cousins, aunts, and uncles.

When I was twelve years old, my father appointed me secretary-treasurer of the family, creating a situation in which a father came to his teenage son for spending money! That went on for years. Dad bought me a small Smith-Corona typewriter to help in handling family correspondence before I had learned to type. He also constructed homemade shelves with cubbyholes to hold letters and information related to family programs and appearances. I accumulated many documents about the family during our singing career, and these were later placed in a metal file cabinet.

In my files I kept carbon copies of all correspondence and folders with numerous newspaper clippings, magazine articles, radio scripts, songbooks, and sheet music—items which convinced me that, indeed, the family story was an important part of "our American heritage." Not to put it in writing would be negligence on my part, inasmuch as I had access to the materials and had already shared much of it with my parishioners in sermons and newsletters.

To my parents, who remain much alive in spirit; to my sister, Betty, who built her own singing career apart from the family; and to my twin brothers, Bob and Jim, I say, "Thanks for helping me to relive these events and to remain honest in telling them."

To my wife, Evelyn, and to our children—Martha Lynn, Kenneth, Jr., Robin, Wesley, and Christopher, I say, "Thanks for encouraging me to bring this story to life."

To my writer friend, Mike Streissguth, I say, "Thanks for your editing assistance," and to the people at the University Press of Mississippi, I say, "Thanks for printing the story as part of the American Made Music Series, so that readers can learn about the contributions of the Johnson Family Singers." As the following story shows, we began in obscurity and ended in prominence, having become one of the eminent singing families of America.

INTRODUCTION

Southern gospel music is one of the most pervasive, and yet least chronicled, types of American music. If you were to travel through the South—or for that matter, the Midwest—and go into the homes, the schoolhouse auditoriums, the small town churches, the county fairs, and survey the kinds of music the people themselves were singing and listening to, you would in most cases find that the music of choice would be gospel. To be sure, here and there you would find an occasional banjo player, or a bluegrass band, or a square dance band, or a blues singer, or a jazz band, or a barbershop quartet, but for every one of those you found, you would find a half dozen gospel groups. Though it seldom shows up in Wal-Marts and K-Marts, or on network television, gospel is, and has been, the music of choice for millions of average working-class Americans. It is a sleeping giant on the cultural landscape.

Not surprisingly, far too little has been written about southern gospel. It is about the only genre of southern music that lacks a comprehensive history, and it is rare to find a detailed account of any of the major figures in the music. This is one of the reasons that Kenneth Johnson's *The Johnson Family Singers: We Sang for Our Supper* is such an important account. To any fan of gospel music, the Johnson Family needs no introduction; their records and radio shows made them one of the dominant groups in the 1940s, one of the first groups to show that gospel singing could be professionalized and could appeal to an audience well beyond the South. Taken by itself, their story would be a key chapter in any history of gospel; but this version of their story is even more remarkable in that it is a first-person, inside account, told by one of the major figures in the group, Kenneth Johnson. Through his evocative, detailed narrative, we actually learn what it was like for a family to struggle up through rural poverty and to take their music into the turbulent mass media of Depression-wracked America.

The handful of other books about gospel groups—such as the Speer Family, the Blackwood Brothers, George Beverly Shea, Jimmie Davis—have been self-proclaimed "spiritual autobiographies," designed to use biography as a testimony to faith. Often such accounts are rather short on details, and rather long on sermonizing. Too often they are ghost-written by professional writers who did not live the events they described. This is definitely not the case with Kenneth Johnson's book. While he is himself very serious about his religion, and respects a good sermon as well as anyone, he lets the facts speak for themselves here. After all, he explains early on that his job in the Family was to act as the secretary and business manager, and he shares with us many of the details about how the Family actually made its living. For the first time in any gospel book, we get some indication about how many records a "hit" sold in the 1940s, how much money radio work brought in, and how much could be gained from teaching a rural singing school. So too does Kenneth have a fine eye for detail of the North Carolina landscape that he and his family grew up in. We learn that Pa Johnson got his first recording contract by selling a rabbit he had trapped; we discover that, even after the family was broadcasting on the radio, they had to resort to picking cotton to make ends meet. If he writes with rare conviction, it is because he was there, and he is speaking from first-hand experience.

When Pa Johnson hitchhiked his way to Dallas, Texas, in 1938 to attend the Stamps-Baxter singing school, it marked not only the start of the Johnson Family singing tradition. He was inserting himself into the very mainstream of the southern gospel movement. Unlike all other forms of southern vernacular music, gospel music was a creature not of record companies or radio, but of the song book publishers. The first modern publisher was the James D. Vaughan Company of Tennessee; Vaughan began to publish books about 1903 and hit upon the idea of having quartets travel around to publicize his songs. One of his pupils, V. O. Stamps, joined forces with J. R. Baxter, Jr., about 1926, to form the Stamps-Baxter Company. Though there were dozens of lesser companies, by the mid-1930s these two companies had become the dominant giants in the field.

By the time Pa Johnson went to Dallas, though, the tail was wagging the dog. The quartets (or quintets, or trios) that had been employees of the publishers were finding out that they could go out on their own and perform as early country or pop groups did. So while Pa ordered his music rudiments chart and followed the old tradition of teaching singing schools, he also followed the new tradition of organizing an independent singing group. Though they may not have known it at the time, the Johnsons found themselves on one of the great watersheds in gospel music, one where the music was changing from a participatory congregational singing to an audience watching a specialized group of experts sing.

Along the way in *The Johnson Family Singers* we get glimpses of this early world of pioneer gospel singers and of the world of early radio. We meet the Rangers, the famed quartet that toured on bicycles; the LeFevre Trio; country music figures like the Carter Family and Arthur "Guitar Boogie" Smith; and the Johnsons' announcer, the well-known North Carolina personality Grady Cole (not to be confused with the Georgian Grady Cole, who wrote "Tramp on the Street"). There is a marvelous account of Betty Johnson's foray into the pre–rock and roll pop music scene of the 1950s.

All in all, this is a marvelously rich book, a rare account of one of the most versatile and unusual family singing groups in modern times. It would be wonderful if each of the great gospel groups could find a chronicler as conscientious and as talented as Kenneth Johnson. But that too would be unlikely, and we should be grateful for what Kenneth Johnson has produced and for his willingness to share it. He has done his family proud.

Charles Wolfe

THE JOHNSON FAMILY SINGERS

AN UNCOMMON BEGINNING

When Ed Sullivan died on October 13, 1974, the headline of the obituary notice in the *New York Times* read, "Ed Sullivan is Dead at 73; Charmed Millions on TV." We Johnsons were among the millions whom Sullivan charmed. We were also privileged on two occasions to appear on his popular Sunday night program, *The Ed Sullivan Show*. We first appeared on March 2, 1958; then, because of the enthusiastic reception, Ed invited us back four weeks later, on Easter Sunday.

An estimated forty-five to fifty million people sat riveted before their TV sets on Sunday nights during the long-running Sullivan series—September 25, 1955, to June 6, 1971. Famous for his poker face, Sullivan was neither witty nor consciously entertaining, yet he had an unusual way of creating audience empathy as he directed the cameras at an array of talented people. So rarely did he smile in his early days of camera fright that he came to be known as "the great stone face."

My sister, Betty, who had left the family group in 1952 to pursue a singing career on her own, had made several solo appearances on the Sullivan show before my family was invited there in 1958. When Ed Sullivan first knew about Betty, he did not realize that she came from a singing family in a place called Possum Walk, North Carolina! In a conversation with Ed one day, Betty mentioned something about her beginnings. He was intrigued and asked her to get the family together for one of his shows.

Betty enthusiastically conveyed the invitation to family members, promising a one-thousand-dollar gift to my church if I could arrange to be away for a Lenten weekend. We flew to New York for the Saturday rehearsal. (When the second appearance came on Easter Sunday, my congregation reversed the order of worship and Sunday School, which allowed me to catch a noon plane and arrive in time for the dress rehearsal.) As Sullivan's lights flashed and his cameras snapped on, I thought to myself, "We're small-time performers no more." In those March appearances, we were lined up with such notables as the Chicago Ballet Company, Carol Burnett, Conrad Hilton, Maurice Chevalier, and Guy Lombardo and his Royal Canadians.

Two months after our appearances, Sullivan told the *Charlotte Observer*: "As you know, I've had the Johnsons on twice. And they're just wonderful. They make such a darn nice picture together—Ma, Pa, that son who's a minister, the twins and Betty. They not only have talent, but they have winning personalities. Yes, I definitely plan to have them back as a group. The reports on them were just outstanding. They got a tremendous audience reaction."

The story of the Johnson Family Singers began in the midsection of North Carolina, called the Piedmont, an area where, at the turn of this century, our relatives barely eked out a living from the mills' spindles and the clay fields. I have always envied people who can trace their roots back to the *Mayflower* or the Revolution or even the Civil War. For us Johnsons, fate limits our knowledge of relatives on both sides of the family tree.

My mother's father, Louis Edgar Craven, is the earliest relative I can find on the maternal side of our family. Known to his friends as Eddie, Grandfather Craven died from a gunshot wound in a hunting accident in the fall of 1907, leaving behind a thirty-year-old widow and six children: Effie, Lessie, Willie, Kenneth, Alma, and Lydia. The fourth born, Mattie, had died in infancy.

Lydia, our mother, was a few months old when her father died. In researching her history, I could not determine whether he had been an adopted or an illegitimate child. All I could establish was that his mother, Cornelia, first married a man named Stout; then, later in life, after her sixty-fifth birthday, she married Giles Smith. The use of Cornelia's maiden name, Craven, suggests either a foster or illegitimate beginning for her son, Eddie.

My maternal grandmother, Roberta Adelaide Brady Craven, married LeRoy Chrisco a year or so after Edgar's tragic death. He was eleven years her junior, and, at the youthful age of twenty-one, took on a wife and six children! Before he smashed his foot in the cotton mill at the age of forty-six, resulting in a deadly blood clot, he added eight more children to the brood.

I have heard different views expressed about the Chrisco marriage. The Chriscos themselves insist that LeRoy's outbursts were more bark than bite. The Cravens, on the other hand, argue that their stepfather was a harsh taskmaster. Though he was sometimes immature, his behavior was counterbalanced in the marriage by Berta's long-suffering and selfless spirit. Fortunately, his sense of responsibility did increase, and his older wife and the children helped to nurture this growth.

Early in the marriage, LeRoy seemed unable to decide whether to make a living in the cotton mill or on the farm, and the family moved back and forth between the two. Once when they had harvested a good crop, LeRoy bought a new car rather than some much-needed clothes for the children. He was a better manager of crops than of money. As a result, the older Craven children secured mill jobs as soon as possible, helping to supplement the family income.

In the spring of 1977, when my mother visited our parsonage in Mooresville, North Carolina, my two younger sons turned on their tape recorder and interviewed her about the early days. "When I was a little girl in Randolph County," one of her stories began, "we took all of our old clothes and tore up the best pieces into strips. We would then tack them together with a needle, wrap them in a large ball, put them in a tow bag, and take them out to a business that made 'carpet.' Why, we had 'carpet' all over the house, even on the staircase!"

Life in the Craven-Chrisco household was a very creative experience. My mother told the grandsons how her mother would make her annual supply of soap by firing up a wash pot in the back yard. She would then let the ingredients—which included lard and Red Devil lye—boil for a time before letting them cool and harden. Later she would cut the batch of soap into squares and use them for washing and cleaning.

When I was growing up, Mother would tell me about her mother storing dill pickles in a keg. They were kept in a mixture of water and salt, covered by a cloth top. When pickles were needed, my grandmother would take them out of the keg, slice them, and put them in a flour sack. The pickles would then be taken to a nearby creek so that "branch water" could be run over them! I always marveled at how pickles with that kind of treatment could end up with a dill taste. Obviously, streams in that day were not polluted as they are now.

In the fall, family members gathered persimmons and placed them on a board in the barn, where the fruits would dry out and shrivel. Then they would be passed off at Christmastime as "raisins"! Other cherished holiday delicacies included walnut kernels covered with molasses-coated popcorn. Christmas goodies were not "hung by the chimney with care" in stockings but were placed in a shoe box under the tree.

"We had lots of cotton to pick," Mother told my sons. "Since cotton didn't mature until late fall, we'd pull off the bolls after school and put them in a big checkered sheet that we had placed on the porch. After supper, we would bring in the sheet full of cotton bolls, pick out the cotton, and throw the burrs in the fireplace. Neighbors would come in to help and the boys would try to charm the girls with sticks of chewing gum."

In addition to housework, Mother took her turn cutting wood and starting fires in the fireplace. (This accounted for her lifelong interest in fireplaces and her use of the fireplace for supplementary heat and cooking during the energy crisis toward the end of her life.) She claimed to be able to "outsaw" most men. Having been at one end of the crosscut with her during my younger days, I can verify that she was not unduly boastful about her physical prowess.

"We didn't have much," Mother confessed, "but we were happy. For instance, we had two school dresses which we had to wear for a whole week. The minute we got home from school, we'd take off the one we were wearing and wear the other around the house. As for Sunday, we had only one dress outfit, which we wore every Sunday to church, unless we had to stay at home because of rain."

My mother not only helped with the children in her own family but also developed a warm friendship with the lady from whom they rented. She would visit this neighbor and help with the churning. In return, the woman would give her a gallon of fresh buttermilk and a pound of butter to take home, which gave Mother a real sense of achievement and brought pleasure to other family members.

The Craven and Chrisco children would sometimes combine forces to clean up new ground, in return for which they could grow crops for two years without paying any rent. Today tractors and bulldozers have supplanted muscle power in such operations, just as television and travel have replaced the bonfires that provided family entertainment.

"My mother used to send me to the store every other week to get the things we needed for the home," Mother told my sons. "We swapped our eggs for what we needed in the kitchen—things like sugar, salt, pepper, and coffee. We enjoyed that! I shall never forget one time when my mother sent me to the store with an eight-pound lard bucket full of eggs. When I came home, I had a new baby sister! Talk about excitement, we really had it in our house."

Alma and Lydia, who were separated in age by two years, would often have visits from boyfriends at the same time. On wintry nights, stepfather LeRoy would allow them to use only one bucketful of coal for the living room fireplace. He was trying not to penalize the girls or their suitors but to conserve fuel! Whatever his reasoning, it made him very unpopular with his stepdaughters. Aunt Alma once referred to my mother as "one of those stubborn Cravens." No doubt there was a certain doggedness about her, shaped in part by the poverty and insecurity of her childhood.

When LeRoy's strong will and my mother's temper collided, something had to give. It was only natural, therefore, for the Craven children to get out on their own as soon as possible. For my mother, a sense of freedom came with visits to Uncle Kenneth in Greensboro, where she did his housekeeping. Because of the absence of any stringent labor laws then, she was able as a young teenager to get a spinning job in the local cotton mill.

Gone was the opportunity for my mother to complete her education; economic survival won out, with the result that Mother did not attend school beyond the third grade. Lydia Florence Craven had been born on January 21, 1907, in Ramseur, North Carolina, on the eastern edge of Randolph County. The story of my father's birth and upbringing is a study in contrast. My mother was the last born in a large family, with all of the attending notice and adulation of other children, friends, and neighbors. Dad, on the other hand, was born without fanfare and raised by an aunt and uncle in an obscure village, away from his biological father and mother.

In the adjacent county of Chatham, Jesse Deverin Johnson was born in the coal-mining village of Cumnock on February 2, 1905, Ground Hog Day. His mother, Minnie Florence Seymour, was a frightened and embarrassed practical nurse from Raleigh, who had come to her half-sister, Mary Johnson, at Cumnock for help in delivering her baby. At the turn of the twentieth century, nursing was a profession already held in low regard, but for a nurse to be pregnant and unmarried was even worse! Although today's out-of-wedlock births are common happenings in most communities, with little or no social stigma, such was not the case in 1905.

Today Cumnock, North Carolina, is barely a speck on the map, but at one time it was a place of importance. During the Civil War, it was a major source of coal for the Confederacy, particularly for the blockade runners and naval vessels operating off the Carolina coast.

Twenty years before the signing of the Declaration of Independence, colonial settlers had been active in the southern part of Chatham County, North Carolina, which in 1908 became part of Lee County. There they found a rich vein of coal. For years mining flourished in the area. Later entrepreneurs attempted to operate iron furnaces. For a brief time, the ironworks were taken over by the fledgling American government, but in 1777 they were sold to John Willcox, who tried to operate them under private ownership. The following year, Mr. Willcox sold the ironworks at auction in Hillsborough; two years later, they were ruined by flooding.

Coal mining fared better than iron works in the land of my father's birth. In mid-nineteenth-century America, steam was beginning to catch on and the demand for coal was growing. In 1855 the most famous coal mine in the area, the so-called Egypt Mine, was opened. Egypt (now Cumnock) began as a small settlement, then called LeGrange, on the plantation of Peter Evans, who gave it the name Egypt apparently because local inhabitants who came to buy corn reminded him of the people of biblical times who went to Egypt to buy "corn" from Joseph (Genesis 42: 1–2). Mr. Evans did not seem to know that what Americans call corn is indigenous to this country, and that the reference in the Old Testament is to some other grain.

The Egypt Mine (originally in Chatham County) ultimately reached a depth of 460 feet and returned a large quantity of coal of good quality. In 1895 it was renamed Cumnock, apparently after someone involved in the mining industry. The expected boom in mining, however, did not materialize. Life at Cumnock was difficult in an era of depression, and hardship was shared by all. Numerous explosions and other accidents caused the mine to close for good in 1929.

When Minnie Seymour arrived at her half-sister's home in Cumnock in January 1905, she was welcomed as a family member and allowed to remain there until the birth of her child. She was twenty-seven at the time, not much older than some of Jack and Mary Johnson's four children (the youngest, Martha, was unmarried and lived at home). The Johnson family became participants in an unusual event—the birth of a baby who would later adopt their name and become the father and originator of an important singing family.

Mystery will probably always surround the identity of my paternal grandfather. Minnie shared the secret only with her sister in Raleigh, Fannie Seymour Porter, who died in the late 1950s and whom I met several years before her death when I was a young adult. Her only comment to me on the subject was "You'd be proud of your grandfather." This led my sister and brothers and me to speculate that our grandfather may have been a professional person, perhaps a doctor or a lawyer. Had he been one of my grandmother's patients? Where did she meet him?

An elderly black midwife, "Aunt" Sophia, was called in to assist in the delivery of Minnie's baby. Birth certificates were not required then, and I decided to file a delayed certificate of birth for my father in the early 1960s. As part of the supporting evidence for his birthdate, I secured an affidavit from his mother, dated September 13, 1958. The name given by her was "Jesse Deverin Johnson." Once in a conversation about the name, she told me that my father's middle name had come from a character named Delwin in a novel she had read. How his name got transformed into Deverin or the reason that Jesse was chosen will probably remain a mystery, along with the name of his father.

After several days, Dad's mother returned to Raleigh, where she resumed her nursing career. A faded letter of recommendation about her nursing, written by a doctor on May 24, 1905, was kept by my grandmother across the years. It was given to me by her daughter, Frances, a few years before her death:

Raleigh, N. C.
May 24th, 1905

To Whom It May Concern—
I have employed Miss Minnie Seymour several times as a caretaker for the sick, and I have always found her an exceeding efficient and thoroughly trustworthy woman. She is tactful and is always well-liked. I commend her for her special work most heartily.
S. Delia Dixon Carroll, M. D.

Still later in 1905, the coal mining operation at Cumnock halted again because of an explosion, at which time Jack and Mary Johnson loaded a wagon with their belongings and Minnie's infant son and headed for Greensboro, North Carolina. Arriving there, they moved into a house at Print Works, the site of a carpet mill on the northeast edge of the city. Unable to carry their pig along, they traded it to a neighbor for a shotgun, which was later given to my father, who eventually gave it to me. Jack secured a job in a local mill and Mary took in washing to supplement the family income. As a small youngster, I visited "Granny" Johnson, whom I especially remember for her fishing in the White Oak Mill pond. Her snuff-dipping made quite an impression!

Dad also told me the story of another pig. His mother had sent it to him in a small box, and its coming from her made it a special gift. He grew very fond of the little animal and was sad to see it grow up and eventually be slaughtered for meat. He also remembered going with his uncle Jack to Wilson's store.

Mary Johnson told him in later years about the time Minnie came to Greensboro to get her son. She had become engaged to a farmer named Fred Shellem, who lived near Denver, North Carolina, and they had decided to take the boy with them, pretending that he was their son. This gesture was important to my father, because it was evidence that he had not been forgotten by his mother. However, Jack and Mary had become attached to the child and felt that, since they had clothed and fed him, they should be allowed to keep him.

Quite an argument ensued over Minnie's attempt to take the boy, and this conflict over Jesse's custody kept the sisters apart for the rest of their lives. Minnie and Fred became reconciled to the fact that they would have to go on with their lives, caring for the two daughters born to them, Elizabeth and Frances. The girls didn't know they had a brother until they were young adults, when my father made a surprise visit to the Denver farm. His mother was quite upset about my father's revelation to them.

Mary Johnson's youngest daughter, Martha, enrolled my father in the White Oak school. His social adjustments there did not constitute the most pleasant of childhood memories. He was frequently in trouble with his classmates and teachers. However, his friendship with Edgar Nease, who kept the larger boys from hurting him, lasted for many years. Edgar later became an outstanding preacher and administrator in the Western North Carolina Conference of the Methodist Church. He was appointed superintendent of the Charlotte District, and, on August 31, 1951, he signed my local preacher's license when I entered the Methodist ministry.

When my father was in the second grade, an incident occurred which would be significant for him and, later, for the musical family he would lead. At the time Martha Johnson enrolled him in the first grade, she told the teacher that his name was Jesse Seymour, but my father didn't like the sound of his last name. Classmates teased him mercilessly, calling him "Seymour-I-see-you" or "Jesse-I-see-who?" So, when his second-grade teacher asked him for his name, he answered, "Jesse Johnson"! The name stuck. By this time, his aunt Mary had become "Mama," and, when we were youngsters, my sister and brothers and I referred to her as "Granny" Johnson. Uncle Jack remained "Uncle Jack" to my father. Looking back upon the Johnson appellation more than fifty years later, we realize just how close the Johnson Family Singers came to having a different surname!

After two years in the White Oak school, my father transferred to the Proximity school, which was nearer to his home in Print Works. He had not been there long, however, when an argument ensued between him and a fellow student named Cobb. Dad told me how he found an old soaked corncob and threw it at the other boy. It hit Cobb in the throat and temporarily knocked him out of breath. Dad was expelled over the incident. When he arrived home and told his story to "Mama" Johnson, she responded sympathetically, "I don't blame you at all, Jesse, for leaving!" Since Jack and Mary could neither read nor write, schooling was not a priority concern for them.

When Dad began the fourth grade at White Oak school, Jack and Mary moved to a house on 18th Street, a street that led to Thacker's Dairy. While schooling was fairly normal, his relations with Martha at home grew worse. My father tried to think of ways of improving the situation, claiming, "Martha was mean to me. . . . She started telling Mama things I didn't do." He rebelled dramatically one morning during breakfast with his family. In recounting the incident, he told me how he had finished eating first and excused himself from the table. He went into the living room, where he turned on an old Edison cylinder player. While it was playing, he quietly slipped out of the house, making his way across the hedge and onto a macadamized road a mile or so away, where he had prearranged to meet some buddies. Earlier he had told these friends of his plans to run away, so they met him at the bridge with their promised meat biscuits to help him on his way.

At the tender age of eleven, my father chose "flight" rather than "fight" in his attempt to be his own person. "I walked into town," he told me. "I had heard about people who rode the 'blinds' of the train. I didn't know what it was all about, but I got up between two passenger cars barefooted—one foot on the ledge of one car and the other foot on another car. When the train stopped in High Point, I got off because the strain of standing barefooted between those two cars was almost unbearable. No sooner did I hop off the train than a policeman grabbed me and took me down to the police station."

"Boy, didn't you know you were riding dangerously back there on that train?" The policeman scowled at my father, who didn't answer because he thought he was riding the train the right way. "If you're gonna ride a train," the officer counseled, "don't ever get between two boxcars. That's too dangerous. Get up behind the coal tender." His final words to Dad were "Don't you ever let me see you again in this town! The next time I catch you like this, I'm gonna put you in jail."

"Night was beginning to fall as I sneaked back to the tracks," my father said, continuing his story. "Later, I caught another train to Salisbury. This time I got behind the coal tender. But what I didn't know was that on the different stops the firemen watered down the coal, which meant that the waters and cinders and dust came splattering back on me! When I got off in Salisbury, I was real dirty and hungry. I had long before finished my meat biscuits—those I hadn't dropped along the way!

"In Salisbury, I remember going to a house where a black family lived. They invited me in, gave me some soap and water to wash up and some food to eat. I told them I was planning to ride another train out of town. The man's son was a car-knocker [brakeman] in the yards, so he directed me to an empty boxcar. I couldn't open it. I was too little and it was too high up. He opened it for me and I crawled in.

"The train wound up somewhere in Georgia. I tried getting a job, but I was too little. So I caught another freight train headed back toward North Carolina. During a car shift, I got off at a place called Coward, South Carolina, and went to a nearby grocery store. Leo Matthews ran the store. He asked me, 'Boy, where you from?' I told him, 'I just came from Georgia'—which was the truth. 'But where do your folks live?' he persisted. 'I don't have no people,' I replied. 'Are you sure you didn't run away from the reformatory school over at Florence?'

" 'What's a reformatory school?' I asked. He explained it was a place for runaway boys. He then said that since I didn't have any family, he would treat me as one of his kids. He also promised to give me a job working in his store. Luckily he had an old-fashioned soda fountain and he let me jerk sodas. I drank so much raw coke that I became sick. He taught me how to drive his Model-T Ford.

"After working in the store for awhile, I met Mr. Matthews's brother, Luther, who was a farmer. I liked him because he was always nice to me when he came in the store. I decided I'd leave the store and work for Luther in tobacco. I didn't work too much because I became ill with malaria. Eventually, though, I started working in the tobacco.

"One day, Luther sent me to a neighbor's house to get a load of tobacco sticks. Instead of getting the sticks, though, I left—leaving the mule and sled standing in a neighbor's yard.

"I started walking on the nearby railroad track toward Darlington, about twenty miles north of Coward. There I felt nearly dead. Sick and weak from the effects of malaria, I walked up to a farmhouse and asked for food. A nice lady invited me in, put me to bed, and gave me so much quinine that my ears felt like they were going to pop. During the course of my week's stay there, the lady pried out of me where I was from and wrote a letter to Uncle Jack. After receiving her letter, he caught a train to Darlington and took me back to White Oak."

My father's first runaway episode lasted from late spring to early fall in 1916. Unfortunately, that escapade not only marked the end of any formal schooling but also reinforced some negative behavior patterns, establishing a poor model for dealing with conflict. This kind of running away became a coping mechanism that would haunt him for the rest of his life.

The Chrisco-Craven family lived on 17th Street, a block southeast of the Johnsons, and the families knew about each other. Although my parents didn't meet until a few years later, my father's reputation as a rebellious teenager was well known in the community. "He was the meanest little boy I ever saw," my mother once confided to friends. "He was always walking up the road, throwing rocks."

Dad's behavior in his early teen years resembled that of his late childhood—impetuous, unpredictable, and daring. When a family named Welch moved from Randleman to White Oak, my father developed a close friendship with their son, Clarence. One day Dad talked Clarence, whose nickname was "Cat," into joining him on a freight train ride. The two rebels ended up in Corbin, Kentucky, where they tried to find refuge from the shivering cold in a carload of crossties. As nighttime approached, my father decided he would sleep on top of the crossties. Cat chose to occupy a warmer space at the bottom on one end of the car. Dad begged him to stay close, but Cat insisted on moving to the other end.

Daybreak found the two boys at the switching yard in Corbin. They were still asleep when their car jolted onto a ramp to roll toward a different engine, jamming the crossties toward one end of the car. Dad hollered out to warn Cat of the danger, but his friend didn't answer. He then crawled across the crossties toward the end of the car, fearing the worst.

Dad reported the incident to the brakeman who was passing by and who summoned a crew to unpile the crossties and retrieve the body. Cat's skull was crushed, which meant that he had died instantly. The parents were notified by a railroad official, and his body was shipped back to Greensboro. The Welch family met the casket and took their son's body home until arrangements could be made for burial in Randleman.

In recalling this tragedy, my father told me, "I didn't go to the funeral . . . I felt like I was responsible for his death because I had insisted that he take the trip with me."

From White Oak, the Johnson family moved across town to a house at Pomona, located near the railroad tracks. Dad would often go fishing in a nearby pond belonging to the Pomona Terra-cotta Pipe Co., now Pomona Pipe Products. On one occasion, he had slipped in and hidden himself—or so he thought—behind some willow bushes; he was pulling in perch "right and left." However, a security guard abruptly appeared on the scene. The violation caused my father to be taken to court, but Uncle Jack settled the case with the judge by paying a ten-dollar fine. In those days, that was a lot of money! What disappointed my father most about the incident was the guard's confiscation of the fish, not Uncle Jack's sacrifice in paying a large fine.

At Pomona, Dad met many hobos because of the family's nearness to the railroad tracks. Jack and Mary would often take in a hobo for a meal and overnight stay. My father was fascinated by these guests' tales of adventure. "I would eat up their stories," he told me. "I decided that I would like hoboing, too. So I caught trains to different places. I dreamed of visiting a hobo jungle—and did so on quite a number of occasions."

One hobo jungle which Dad visited was in Big Spring, Texas, in a large wooded area next to the railroad tracks. Scores of hobos lingered there. They begged for food at local stores and homes. A hobo would, for example, go up to a store clerk or housewife and explain that at the previous store or house he had been given some sugar; he would then ask for a donation of coffee! Deception was a law of the jungle. "You were supposed to say that you had gotten something at the previous place, whether you got anything there or not," explained my father.

At Big Spring, the hobos used common pots and pans that would be cleaned and hung up to dry on a tree for the next hobos to use. The owner of that particular jungle had some political pull in town, because the police never raided the place. He was interested in using the manpower of the jungle for his various work projects. He would come on the scene in early morning before the bums awoke and offer them a "grubstake" if they would agree to cut timber or work in the sawmill for a day. Those who accepted the offer could expect $1.00 to $1.50 for their labor.

Surprisingly, not all bums in the hobo jungles came from poor backgrounds. According to my father, some were former businessmen and professionals who had lost their jobs, their money, and even their families. At an earlier time they might have been regarded as community leaders, but, in the jungle, they were simply one among many beggars looking for the next meal.

In 1918, the Johnsons moved to Hillsborough, North Carolina, where, at the tender age of fourteen—still small and frail-looking—my father got a job at the Eno Cotton Mill. His duty was to carry buckets of water from a nearby well to the mill, where the workers used a common dipper. "While they were drinking," my father recalled, "I would wander over to see Minnie Hicks in the weave room, where she taught me to weave."

My father learned another skill at Hillsborough that would later play a role in his singing career. "Wink" Howard, a one-eyed fellow, taught him how to play the guitar. Wink would walk up and down the railroad tracks in early evening, playing his guitar as if in some trance. "A bunch of us boys would hear him coming and follow from behind, watching him play, sing, and drink liquor!"

Later "Mama" Johnson purchased a five-dollar guitar for Jess and, with Wink's help, taught him to play two or three chords. Key changes were created with a capo, a small piece of hard wood clamped across the fingerboard. Later when my family became a singing group, we acknowledged that we never would have made it without Dad's favorite guitar chords and capo! Both later found their way into thousands of radio programs and concert appearances as well as scores of recordings for Columbia and RCA-Victor records.

Unfortunately, the original guitar was later pawned by Dad. In fact, he stopped playing for several years but resumed in the mid-thirties when Mother purchased a Gibson for him with weekly one-dollar installment payments! This guitar was used throughout our music career and was later passed on to my brother Bob, who had it refinished and restrung. Resonant sounds still come from that instrument, as clear today as when my father first played it.

On reaching the age of fifteen, my father felt very self-confident about both his guitar playing and his weaving. It was then that the wanderlust hit him again! So, he caught another freight train—again to Georgia, where he looked for employment. Because of his age and size, though, no one would hire him; he had not even started shaving! Several people advised him to join the navy, so, in 1921 at the age of sixteen, he hopped a boxcar and headed to Rome, Georgia, and then south to Atlanta.

In Georgia's capital city, Dad went to see the navy recruiter, whose first question to him was "Do you have any people living here?" Without blinking an eyelid, my father answered, "I have a cousin." The recruiter said he thought the boy was too light and too young for the navy, but promised that if my father could get some relative to sign for him, he would see what he could do.

Again deception and imagination went to work for my father! No sooner had he left the recruiter's office than he went to a nearby fruit stand and bought a bunch of bananas, all of which he ate to help himself gain weight! Then he went back to the post office building, walked over to a writing desk, and signed the navy application "Henry Johnson." For an address, he gave the name of a nearby street he had noticed, Peachtree, and a fictitious house number for his "uncle." Within an hour, Dad was back in the recruiter's office. "Well," he told the navy man, "my uncle signed it!" The recruiter glanced at the signature and proceeded to process the application.

"You're still mighty slim and puny-looking," he told the young enlistee, "but I'm going to let you in anyway. But," he cautioned, "when you get to Norfolk, I want you to do yourself a favor. I want you to take this slip to a drugstore on the base and get two tablets. They'll cost you twenty-five cents." "But I don't have any money," my father protested. "Never mind," the officer responded, reaching into his pocket for a quarter.

At the Norfolk naval base, the druggist gave Dad the tablets, advising him, "Take these before you cross the water to Hampton Roads. They'll make you sick," he warned. "You'll probably vomit some, but don't worry. Everything'll be all right—eventually!"

The trip to Hampton Roads turned out exactly as the druggist had predicted. At the naval station, Dad was placed in the sick bay. The officers never knew that the pills he had taken had created the nauseous condition. They mistakenly concluded that his weight loss was due to some illness! "I was so skinny they didn't even have clothes to fit me, but I passed the physical with flying colors," he told me. The inoculations didn't help with his recovery, but he eventually finished boot training.

My father had envisioned the navy as a way to see the world; what he had overestimated was his seaworthiness. Before his enlistment, his view of the navy had been shaped by stories he had heard about it in the hobo jungles. He had no intention of trying to "make the world safe for democracy"—the clarion call of President Woodrow Wilson. Nor was he interested in learning any skill offered in naval training. To him, the navy was simply a way of satisfying his wanderlust, part of an unsatisfied search for "belonging" and for a more fulfilled life.

While in the navy, Dad returned to Greensboro for a visit with his uncle Jack and "Mama" Johnson. He also visited White Oak Mill to meet some old friends. At the mill, he spotted an attractive fifteen-year-old spinner, who glanced flirtatiously at him. Since he was dressed in his uniform, he took off his navy kerchief and gave it to the admiring girl, who claimed that she always had wanted one for herself. (Years later, when my twin brothers were quite young and dressed in little navy outfits, a street photographer in Greensboro snapped a picture of my mother holding their hands as she strolled up South Elm Street. Part of her love for this picture, no doubt, was the nostalgia she felt for Dad's navy days.)

After returning to his base at Norfolk, Dad joined the crew of *Destroyer 249* for his maiden voyage across the Atlantic. The ship's first stop was Gibraltar; then it went on to Constantinople (now Istanbul), where it docked for eight months. The crew made several side trips. My father, along with several other sailors, learned about a trip to the Sea of Galilee. For only a few piasters, they could all load onto a small boat and be taken to the place where Jesus walked on water (Matthew 14: 22–27). As the tour guide gave his spiel, Dad felt he had been caught in a tourist trap. "They didn't anymore know where Jesus walked on the water than I did," he told me. Another side trip that broadened Dad's education was to Odessa, Russia. He also mentioned as an unforgettable experience standing watch in the crow's nest during subfreezing weather.

A sailor from Kannapolis, North Carolina, named Ivy joined Dad in an excursion into the Turkish countryside—with the result that *Destroyer 249* pulled out for home without them! Another ship eventually took them to Gibraltar, where they were transferred to an oil tanker, the *Potoka*, and were court-martialed for going AWOL. My father was found guilty of "jumping ship" at Constantinople and was sentenced to ten days in the brig "with nothing to eat," he told me, "but bread and water." The punishment discouraged the young sailor so much that after a second run from Port Arthur, Texas, to Gibraltar and back, he convinced his superiors that he was unfit for the navy. He was discharged because of his incompatibility with naval regulations and requirements. It was the fall of 1922, and he had served for approximately eighteen months.

DIRTY DISHES IN THE EARLY YEARS

Dad's interest in music emerged at an early age, with his exposure to the old Edison cylinder player in the home, containing popular songs of the day, and to Wink Howard's guitar playing on the railroad tracks. He never discussed with me his favorite cylinders or Wink's songs, but he did say both were strong influences in his young life.

After his navy days, he found himself playing a tenor banjo with a group of musicians at Proximity, near White Oak. One fateful day in the fall of 1923, he accepted an invitation from Bill Craven to rehearse with a quartet that was meeting in the Chrisco living room on Gordon Street. "While the quartet was practicing," Dad recounted to hundreds of audiences during our singing days, "I went for a drink of water in the kitchen, where I saw this pretty girl washing dishes.

"Hello there!" my father remembered saying to her. "Let me help you wash those dishes!"

"All right," came her bashful reply, which Dad would imitate in a falsetto voice. People would start laughing, waiting for the punch line: "I didn't wash many dishes then, but I've been washing them ever since!" We children would giggle with laughter as though we were hearing this story for the first time.

Dirty dishes were symbolic of the early part of the Johnson marriage, the presinging days. (By "dirty dishes," I mean those shake-up experiences in the marital ship such as economic hardship, sexual differences, immature development, irresponsible behavior—all of which situations my parents went through in those years.) In March of 1924 they "ran away" to get married in Danville, Virginia. Unable to find anyone to officiate, they traveled back to Reidsville, where, again, the license eluded them. They made a frantic call to Lydia's mother in Greensboro and were assured that "you don't have to run away to get married. . . . Come on back home and get married here."

Having paid a man eight dollars to drive them back to the Chriscos on Gordon Street in Greensboro, Dad obtained a marriage license at the Guilford County courthouse. My grandmother gave her written consent, which was required in order for seventeen-year-old Lydia to be married. They spoke their vows on March 12, 1924, in the family living room, where Dad had attended Bill's quartet practice. He declared to me in a conversation a few years before his death that he had never said, "I do!" during the ceremony. Dad's recollection was that Justice of the Peace Joseph Ritter, who married the couple, had a bad case of the palsy, causing him to shake and nod and resulting in great confusion on the part of the groom as to what his responses should be! "I never said, 'I do,' but I *did*," he told me.

My father's little Proximity band provided the postnuptial music. Dad had briefly played guitar with the local group. After the music celebration was over, the couple walked over to Alma and her husband Earl's house at Print Works for a midnight wedding dinner. They spent the rest of the night there, but it was around two o'clock in the morning before they got to bed. Both rose at five o'clock for their White Oak mill jobs at six—Dad to the weave room and Mother to the spinning room. That was their honeymoon!

Not long after their marriage, Mother contracted a severe case of typhoid fever and was placed in the old St. Leo's Hospital. The nurse there assured her, though, that she would recover and suggested that Dad try to visit her as often as possible. Within a few days, the fever broke and Mother improved.

After she returned home from the hospital, both of my parents went back to their mill jobs but gradually sought greater privacy than they had living with relatives. About this time, Dad joined the Print Works baseball team, where he and "Mutt" Taylor became good friends. Dad was pitcher for the team, Mutt, the catcher. Instead of dealing with the unhappiness brewing at home, Dad used the baseball team as an outlet, following his usual pattern of flight from trouble.

Before long, Dad and Mutt caught a freight train for Columbus, Ohio, where they joined the Car-Knockers baseball team. Mother had cried for several days, trying to prevent a marital breakup, but her tears were not persuasive enough.

Jess had never liked working in a cotton mill; it was too confining, and the pay was low. Baseball was out-of-doors and brought him greater freedom. After making a little money with the Columbus team, he returned to Greensboro. Reluctantly, he told "Mama" Johnson that he had left Liddie, whereupon she informed him that he had better go back because Lydia was going to have a baby! He went back, on the condition that they move from the Chrisco house into their own quarters. Mother agreed.

A small dilapidated house, owned by a lady named Johnson (no relation) in Asheboro, was located at Franklinville in Randolph County. She offered it to my parents rent free if they would keep it up. Berta gave them an old burned-out wood stove, Mary offered some quilts, and they set up housekeeping, such as it was. Dad secured work at a nearby sawmill from a fellow named Smith. Since the lumber business was pretty sluggish at the time, my father was frequently paid off in corn, wheat, chickens, and pigs.

One day a fellow walked by the pigpen my father was building and offered "feed" for the pigs at no cost. The offer turned out to be both a blight and a blessing. While hunting squirrels one day, my father discovered the source of the free feed supply—a whiskey still that was located nearby. Even though the pigs grew rapidly from the still "backings," they were visibly affected by the alcohol content of their food! It took a special measure of chaff to sober them up before slaughter. Dad insisted that the ham had a liquor flavor!

After a few months at Franklinville, my parents moved up to Pole Cat Creek, just south of Greensboro, birthplace of the famed CBS announcer of World War II days, Edward R. Murrow. Meanwhile, Dad had acquired a good used Model T Ford, which he drove to work at the Proximity Mill.

In April 1926, my parents moved back in temporarily with the Chriscos on Gordon Street, where, on the twenty-first of that month, my mother gave birth to her firstborn, a daughter named Doris Louise. She was a beautiful and healthy girl but fretted considerably when she started teething. What my parents didn't know was that she had developed a serious case of colitis. On the night of November 7, 1927, Dad remembered, he put Doris to bed with him and Mother. "She was crying," he told me. "I didn't know she was so sick. I spanked her and she quit crying. The next morning she died."

Again Dad went to Berta Chrisco for help, a pattern he seemed destined to follow during those early years of marriage. His mother-in-law offered to have Doris buried in a plot she owned at Pleasant Ridge Christian Church (now Pleasant Ridge United Church of Christ), where her first husband and several other members of the Brady family were buried. My father took the infant body in a small box-like casket to Pleasant Ridge for the burial.

Hardly had my parents settled down in a four-room house on 21st Street than the Chriscos decided once more to move back to Randolph County. There LeRoy and his family occupied the main house on a sixty-eight-acre farm belonging to his brother-in-law, Edgar Allred. Mother and Dad, not to be left alone in Greensboro, moved into a small house through the woods out behind them.

My father secured a weaving job in Winston-Salem, commuting to his home in Randolph County on the weekends. On February 11, 1928, Dr. Marshall was summoned from nearby Ramseur to deliver a second Johnson baby. In appreciation of Lydia's brother, Kenneth, and the good services of Dr. Marshall, the baby was named Kenneth Marshall Johnson.

"I was sleeping one night when I accidentally turned over in bed and hit your mother's breast with my elbow," Dad told me of yet another family crisis. "The injury caused the breast to rise. Dr. Best was called. He asked for my razor and strap to sharpen it on. Before I knew it, he had cut right down into the breast, letting the puss ooze out. Mrs. Chrisco placed torn sheets and rags around the incision. Because of this," my father said, "you were placed on a bottle." The poor medical procedures of that incident made me wonder how my mother ever survived.

As if a change in the milk source were not enough, I developed some serious head sores. About this time, Earl and Alma closed their small store in Virginia and moved back to the farm with the Chriscos. When Aunt Alma discovered the severity of my illness, she insisted that I see a doctor immediately. She even gave up her cherished five-dollar and ten-dollar gold pieces to pay the bill and obtain some much-needed medicine for me. Years later, Aunt Alma often reminded me, "Marshall, I gave you my gold!"

Commuting to Winston-Salem proved to be too tiresome and expensive for my father, so he quit the job there and went to work painting houses for whatever he could make. The owner would furnish the paint and Dad would do the work for five dollars or ten dollars or for a shoulder of meat—whatever he could get.

Not all was sadness and woe for the family, though. Dad's ingenuity showed itself with some home entertainment he devised. His mail carrier, also a deputy sheriff, was fond of foxhunting. One day while cutting trees, Dad wandered off to a nearby sandbar and made some large tracks in the sand with his axe. On the carrier's next round, Dad reported, "There's some kind of wild animal loose down there in the woods." Later he and the carrier took some dogs to sniff out the creature. My father knew all along that there was no such animal. Even so, the dogs picked up some kind of trail, and the carrier/sheriff never knew the difference.

An old man in the neighborhood would periodically wander off to the back porch of an unoccupied tin-roofed house, where he would meditate and snooze. Dad would let zoom a rock on the tin roof. Despite the annoyance, the man would resume his meditation after my father stopped pestering him. I sensed something of my father's guilt when he confessed these stories to me fifty years later!

Though the nation's economy in the late 1920s was prospering, folks at the bottom of the economic ladder were not doing well. Lawlessness and permissiveness were also rampant. During this period of "bathtub booze," Dad succumbed to the temptation to provide for his wife and young son through illegal means. He did some distilling of his own—in the kitchen! Relatives helped him to erect a homemade kitchen still and eagerly volunteered to be its tasters!

Because he feared detection, Dad bundled up Mother and me and sent us away on yet another move, this time to a house in Chatham County, near Siler City. This move came during the cold winter weeks of 1929, the year the stock market crashed. That year was also devastating for the Johnsons, whose loss was not so much in stocks and bonds as in reputation, a situation that would tarnish our lives for a few years. Disaster appeared innocently enough one night when two of Dad's friends from Greensboro knocked on the door and awakened him.

"Get up, Jess!" one of them said. "We've got a safe here which we want you to help us unlock." Even though it was in the middle of the night, Dad felt that he couldn't turn down one of his former baseball buddies. So, he threw on his clothes and hurried to the barn with his friends. To their surprise, they found that the safe was already open. They also found nothing of value in it, except some papers and a small cylinder, which they later tried unsuccessfully to sell in Siler City.

The darkness of that night was exceeded only by the darkness of the day several weeks later when my father moved us once again back to Greensboro, this time to a large house near Wilson's Store. By this time, his reputation as a bootlegger had reached the ears of local authorities. On Friday, March 8, the police swooped down and searched the house, finding his liquor cache at the bottom of an outside well.

During their search, the police also found the cylinder hone (container), which had been missing from the White Oak Transfer Company. Dad was immediately arrested on a liquor possession charge and taken to the police station, where he was placed in jail to await trial. On Monday, police added a breaking and entering charge to his bill of indictment. As if this weren't enough, three additional breaking and entering charges were leveled against him in subsequent days.

The *Greensboro Daily News* listed the three official charges as follows: the robbery of a safe at the Ford Motor Company (which had taken place four months earlier), breaking and entering Harper's Cafe at McAdoo Heights, and breaking into the office of the Henry Motor Company on Forbis Street, where about $150 was stolen in cash.

My mother gave birth on March 16, 1929, to my younger sister, Betty Jean, while Dad remained behind bars on multiple felony charges. Evidence in the robbery charge did not come to the district court until Wednesday, April 3. Probable cause was found against him and another person and the three cases were bound over to Superior Court. Dad remained in jail, unable to make the one-thousand-dollar bond.

The case was docketed for April 29. The solicitor, J. Frank Spruill of Lexington, whom I came to know when I was a student pastor a couple of years before his death in the 1950s, prosecuted the case the next day.

On May 1, the Greensboro paper headline on page four read: "Two Young White Men Being Tried For Taking Off Safe." With some reluctance, my father discussed the case with me during a visit after Mother's death. If I had not researched the matter previously, I do not believe he would have talked about it.

The pain of this episode was evident in our conversation. Dad asked me not to print the story until after his death and, then, not to print the name of other persons involved in the incident. I have honored both requests. So, in the following newspaper account, I leave the name of the other "young white man" blank, as my father asked:

> Jesse Johnson and ———, who are being tried in Guilford Superior Court, charged with breaking and entering Russell's garage at White Oak, removing the safe therefrom and hauling it away, denied their guilt yesterday. Both pleaded not guilty and ——— took the stand in his denial. In addition to this crime, the defendants are also indicted in Guilford Superior Court on three other counts of breaking and entering.
>
> The safe that was taken from the White Oak garage was later found in the mill race at Franklinville in Randolph County. The defendants are alleged to have told other witnesses, who were produced yesterday, that they hauled the safe off but got it nearly to Franklinville before they found that it had not been locked and that it was empty but for a few tools and some papers worthless to anybody but the owners.
>
> These same defendants are alleged to have broken into the Ford Body Company here and removed several hundred dollars from the safe belonging to that concern. They have also been connected by the police with a number of other safe jobs in this section but have not been tried for these offenses yet.
>
> About the time that the yegg jobs were being pulled in and around Greensboro, Randolph citizens began to fish safes out of their streams, one of them being the one stolen from Russell's garage. As far as it is known, the defendants have no connection with the other safes found submerged in water.

On May 1 my father and his friend were found guilty of breaking and entering Russell's garage in White Oak. Another jury was then impaneled to try them on a case in which they were charged with breaking into the office of the Ford Body Company and taking about five hundred dollars in checks and money. Sentence was withheld in the first case until the jury returned its verdict in the second case. The verdict and sentence did not come until Saturday, May 3.

Fortunately, the *Greensboro Daily News* did not immediately report the outcome of those proceedings. Instead, the May 6, 1929, edition headlined an article about a man who was sentenced to seven years for stealing a horse. The second paragraph of that piece reported that my father and an accomplice who had been convicted of breaking and entering and larceny had been given seven years each in the two cases against them.

Thus the wheels of justice turned ever so slowly over a seven-week period; Dad was convicted on charges of which he was innocent and not convicted on the whiskey possession charge, of which he was guilty! Fifty years later as we were discussing this irony, my father commented on the fate of fellow defendants. "I wouldn't name the other fellows involved. I knew who they were. They were set free. I made the time. I didn't tell on anybody. I came up with the reputation of not being a 'rat.' As a result, I was sentenced to seven years—ball and chain, stripes, and a felony on my record. Conviction of stealing anything over twenty dollars in those days was considered a felony."

The Republicans in 1928 had successfully campaigned with the promise "a chicken in every pot, a car in every garage," but it didn't work out that way for us Johnsons. Dad was sent to the county farm on the eastern edge of Greensboro. Mother was left to fend for herself and two small children. With the benevolent aid of family, friends, and the welfare department, however, she pulled us through. After a few weeks we moved into a small frame house in Bessemer, only a mile or so from the prison farm. One of my earliest recollections is of visiting Dad there.

Just before the stock market crash in October 1929, it was estimated that 50 percent of Americans had annual incomes of less than two thousand dollars, which was then considered the minimum for the basic necessities. We lived below that figure. In retrospect, I marvel at the way Mother provided for us through the Great Depression.

Almost fifty years later, while I was pastor of Central United Methodist Church in Mooresville, North Carolina, I went to visit one of my parishioners, Stamey Ridge, who lived alone in a large two-story farmhouse in the country, not far from his daughter and her family. Six months later, I conducted this man's funeral (he had been taking a lawnmower to a repair shop in Salisbury when he collided with a state truck). In my funeral remarks, I revealed an incredible connection between Stamey and my father. I began, "As some of you know, Stamey Ridge spent most of his working life in the unenviable position of managing a prison camp in Guilford County. In talking with me about his work during a visit in February, he told me he had always tried to practice the Golden Rule with his prisoners. He also told me he did not believe in cursing. He tried to see the best in people and he possessed that remarkable gift of bringing out the best in others."

Only Stamey's daughter, Lib Howard, knew what I was about to say next in my remarks. I had asked her for permission to share a particular story as a tribute to her father. I continued, "There are several stories I could tell to illustrate the virtues in Stamey's life. One especially stands out in my mind. . . . During the early days of the Depression, a young man was assigned to Stamey. Because of this particular inmate's record, Stamey helped him to achieve honor grade, at which time he could drive a prison truck. Eventually when this prisoner was paroled, he was hired by his prison supervisor for a truck job; when this position was terminated, Stamey helped him to get a similar job in Yanceyville.

"I mention this example of compassion in Stamey's life because the prisoner he helped happened to be my father and one of the mouths our brother helped to feed was my own!"

The man who had befriended my father at a very critical point in his life had the son of that prisoner as the officiating minister at his funeral a half-century later.

Also because of Stamey's cooperation, Dad was able to drop by the house occasionally and visit with us. "During one such visit," he confided to me, "your mother became pregnant again!" Because of the family situation, the welfare department combined forces with Mother to secure Dad's parole. He served approximately eighteen months of a seven-year sentence.

During my research for this book, I made an interesting discovery at the department of archives in Raleigh. I found that the defendant convicted along with my father was paroled by Governor O. Max Gardner, who, on December 16, 1930, wrote to the sheriff of Guilford County. The letter read in part:

> The above named prisoner, ———, was convicted at the April Term, 1929, Superior Court of Guilford County of Breaking, Entering and Larceny and sentenced to serve seven years on the county roads.
>
> I am informed that this prisoner was convicted along with another party older than himself and since beginning the service of his sentence the other prisoner has been

paroled. I am informed that this prisoner now has a good prison record and those familiar with the case feel that he should be shown the same consideration as his co-defendant.

The document was signed by Governor Gardner and by O. M. Mull, the governor's executive counsel.

During my father's incarceration, his ingenuity asserted itself again. For one thing, he became a barber to the other prisoners, charging "two bits" for a shave and a haircut (fifteen cents for haircuts and a dime for shaves). Also, he sang in an otherwise all-black quartet. Adjustments, racial or otherwise, never seemed to be a real problem for my father of for any of us during our singing days. Then as always, Dad was able to make the best of a bad situation.

By the time my brothers, Bob and Jim, were born on July 13, 1931, Dad had been paroled, even though it meant being released to poverty again. One bright spot was the invitation from a man named Boatman Clark to Dad for him to take the lead part in a quartet which sang each Sunday at the Bessemer Presbyterian Church.

At a quartet contest at Proximity High School, the group won first prize. It fell Dad's lot to do a solo part in church that Christmas. "We Three Kings" wasn't exactly his type of music, especially for one whose musical experience had been limited to some quartet singing. Nevertheless, he gave the congregation his best effort, with Mother beaming in delight. (Several decades later, when my family was invited by Dr. Embree H. Blackard to sing at Myers Park Methodist Church in Charlotte, we were all decked out in choir robes. I'm sure this brought to Dad's mind that Bessemer solo experience years before.)

If, in the first half of the 1930s, someone had appeared on the scene like Stamey Ridge, who loved people and who took a genuine interest in their well-being, I am confident that the times would not have been as difficult for my parents. The problems that plagued my father resulted from his poor decisions, symbolized by those dirty dishes. Only slowly did he learn that good decisions produce good consequences and bad decisions produce bad consequences.

During this period, my parents' nuptial ship was again shaken, causing them by mutual consent to separate. Dad agreed to take the twins, Bob and Jim, while Betty and I remained with Mother.

I cannot remember ever hearing my parents argue about their marriage or anything else. I never saw any abuse, between them or toward us. I believe that the separation may have been as much for economic reasons as anything else. As always, Dad was chasing rainbows. The grass always looked greener on the other side. Jobs were not plentiful and those which he found were not satisfying or fulfilling. Then, too, the problem of wanderlust continued to resurface.

For a brief time, we continued living out on the Reidsville Road, where we had moved from Bessemer. After Dad and the twins left, Mother moved Betty and me to an apartment on South Elm Street.

Because of the trauma of my parents' separation, Betty and I developed a close relationship that continues to this day. Only thirteen months apart in age, we were pleased that Mother decided not to start me in school until my sister could begin with me. This meant that when we enrolled in David Caldwell Elementary School I was seven and she was six, but we were together, which is what seemed important at the time. When the principal at Caldwell tried to separate us into different first grade rooms, I cried until she put us together again!

Betty and I were fortunate in having Miss Nannie White as our teacher. She gave us a sense of stability by teaching us in our first three grades, merely changing rooms with us each year. This met not only our educational needs but our emotional ones as well. After her retirement, Miss White moved to Birmingham, Alabama, where in the ninetieth decade of life she wrote her memoirs. She lived to be a hundred.

Dad was in and out of Greensboro during this time, often leaving the twins with Grandmother at White Oak. Once he took them to Opelika, Alabama, where they stayed in a Catholic convent. The parish priest was very thoughtful and kind, according to my father. He wanted to adopt the twins. For a period of time, Dad sold advertising for liturgical books used in the Catholic services.

One incident on April 2, 1936, almost ended the Johnson Family Singers before we ever got started. Betty had gone out in the late afternoon to help a friend deliver newspapers. The twins were at Grandmother's. Dad was away somewhere. Only Mother and I were in the apartment on South Elm Street in the late afternoon when I noticed the sky growing darker and darker. I stepped to the window and saw a funnel-shaped cloud hovering over the street. It looked threatening, as if something terrible were about to happen.

Earlier in the day, a raging tornado had hit Cordele, Georgia, killing twenty-three and leaving a thousand people homeless. The erratic spring storm, reaching a wind velocity of eighty to ninety miles an hour at times, roared out of the southwest corner of Georgia and hedgehopped crazily to the northeast. The tornado then turned north after devastating Cordele. Other towns were hit by the deadly storm en route to Greensboro, but it was the city that suffered most. There Mother and I hovered nervously in a third-floor apartment as the ominous winds blew.

The *Greensboro Daily News* carried pictures and stories of the event. A front-page article in the *New York Times* the next day gave the grim statistics: eleven known dead, more than a hundred injured, and property damage in excess of a million dollars. Later figures were revised upward, showing that thirteen people had been killed and a hundred forty-four injured (fifty-six of them seriously), with damage estimated at two and a half million dollars. Power was shut off in the city, and the National Guard was called out as a protective measure.

The storm hit at 7:05 p. m. and lasted only seven minutes—but what a terrifying seven minutes! One woman down at the end of the hall from us screamed as she was cut by broken glass. I remember Mother grabbing me and jumping what seemed to be a flight of steps just as the tornado hit. Meanwhile, I heard sirens and crashing noises about us. Mother and I huddled on a landing between the third and second floors with four or five other people. Dust stifled our breathing. I could hear the soft rain begin to hit the street outside. Somebody asked, "Anybody got a match?" Another person did and lit it. I glanced about at the soot-covered faces as we cautiously edged our way down a flight of steps through the debris to the street below. Firemen, policemen, and ambulances were arriving, caring first for the injured and dying.

Eventually a policeman came over to us and with his flashlight helped Mother and me to cross the live wires in the street. We were led up Elm Street to an emergency Red Cross shelter which had been hastily set up in a building next to the railroad tracks. Happily, Betty found us at this location later in the night after a frantic and frightful search.

Nowadays as I travel through "Olde Greensborough"—that section of Elm Street south of the old Jefferson Standard building down to Lee Street—I am reminded when I see the 610 1/2 address, now covered with layers of paint, that the top floor at the north end of the block had to be completely removed as a result of the tornado damages. Olde Greensborough, including our former apartment building, was placed in the National Register of Historic Places in June of 1982.

John Wesley, founder of "the People called Methodists," often referred to himself as "a brand plucked from the burning" because neighbors had formed a human ladder to rescue him from the fire that destroyed the old rectory in Epworth, England, when he was a small child. The Greensboro tornado lacked that kind of historical significance, but I have always felt that the lives of two Johnsons were spared for their mission in the world. I have never ceased being grateful to God for that mercy which spared our lives during a seven-minute ordeal. Mother and I were definitely "plucked" from a disaster.

The quality of our days in mid-Depression times was aptly described by President Franklin D. Roosevelt, who, in his second inaugural address said, "I see one-third of the nation ill-housed, ill-clad, and ill-nourished." Added to these physical miseries for our family was the burden of marital separation, which was not a pleasant experience for either of my parents. Their extramarital relations were dismal failures, also. Occasional court hearings and nonsupport charges made bad matters worse. In a visit with Effie, Mother's sister, arrangements were made for my parents to reconcile their differences and go back together again. Just before that reunion, however, Dad made one final foray on the rails—one that was to become a turning point in bringing the family together and establishing a music career that would make the Johnson Family Singers a household name from coast to coast.

Dad's constructive "flight" came in the summer of 1938. He had always admired the Stamps-Baxter Quartet from Dallas, Texas, and whenever the group appeared in the area, he would go to hear them. He also attended singing schools conducted by Frank Stamps (these were usually held in church sanctuaries for a couple of hours each weekday evening). He became excited about the big singing school in Dallas and made plans to go there alone by hitchhiking rides.

On his way, Dad stopped off in Terrell, Texas, or, to put it more accurately, he was let off in Terrell. "While standing on a street corner waiting for another ride," he recalled, "I overheard two men talking about some old gentleman who had died. They were trying to get a quartet together to sing for the funeral. I stepped over and interrupted, saying, 'I'll be more than glad to sing with you boys.' I then went to the funeral and helped those fellows with the service."

After the funeral, Dad started talking with the funeral director, who asked about his circumstances. My father explained that he was on his way to the singing school at the Stamps-Baxter Music Company in Dallas, provided they would let him attend on credit. The funeral director then provided overnight lodging in his sister's home and personally took my father to Dallas the next day, asking the Stamps-Baxter people to defer payment until Dad could send the money.

Dad took all the courses that were offered—singing, music theory, and conducting. When the school ended, he hitchhiked back to Greensboro and told us about it with great excitement. "We'll have to go there some day," he said. I learned from Dad's enthusiasm that happiness is a by-product of music, and would especially be so when a family sang together. Our music career was about to be launched.

VAGABONDS OF SONG

The term "vagabond" (moving from place to place) aptly describes the life of my family during the period 1938 to 1942, the early years of our singing career. We lived in six places, with the children attending seven different schools in two states. While we were able finally to reach our goal of becoming singers on powerful WBT, the fifty-thousand-watt CBS station in Charlotte that commanded hundreds of thousands of listeners up and down the eastern seaboard, we had been "laid off" for a few months before the 1942 move to Charlotte, at which time we became staff singers at WBT and then worked continuously for the next nine years.

Dad alone had attended the Stamps-Baxter School of Music in Dallas, Texas, in the summer of 1938. When he returned to our apartment in Greensboro, he ordered a music chart published by Ruebush-Kieffer in Dayton, Virginia.

I learned only recently the story of Ephraim Ruebush, a Union soldier, rescuing a bright young southern musician named Aldine S. Kieffer from a Union camp for prisoners of war. Over the next few years, these two men became brothers-in-law and business partners. In the late 1860s, they established a publishing company in New Market, Virginia, which printed books of sacred and gospel songs. Until then, such songbooks had been written in a four-note system called sacred harp. The Ruebush-Kieffer books contained songs written on a seven-note scale that provided a completely different style of harmony and sound. Ruebush and Kieffer also published the chart which Dad used to teach us to read music. Those shaped notes were magic to our young eyes and ears!

Family members learned to sing songs by first singing the notes. To my ten-year-old mind, the shape of the note on the staff indicated its pitch. Those notes, in ascending order, always began with "do," which looks like a triangle, followed by a wash-pot-looking "re"; "mi" is diamond shaped; "fa" is the left half

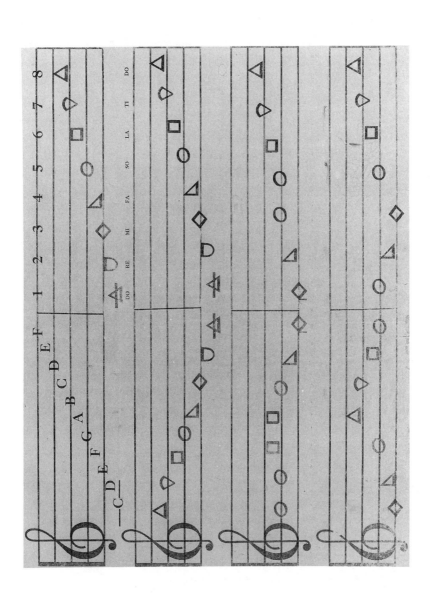

of a square, left top to right bottom; "sol," always round; "la," a block; "ti," an ice-cream cone, and back to "do."

To sing a line of shape-note music was both simple and easy. The shape of the note reinforced the note's position on the lines and spaces of the staff and helped the singer to identify the proper pitch. Once we had sung a hymn or gospel song through with the notes, we then switched to the words. Never shall I forget singing the notes of my first hymn, "Footsteps of Jesus." To this day, I can sing it by shape note from memory: "mi, mi, mi, mi, re, do, la, la, sol; sol, mi, do, re," etc. On the other hand, singing "round notes"—aided only by their position on the staff—was more difficult.

Anyone driving up in the middle of a summer day in the early 1940s to the family porch might have found our neighbor, Clarence Proctor, my father, and me going through the Stamps-Baxter Quartet's *Anchored Faith* (1943) or James D. Vaughan's *Singing Star* (1941)—singing the notes! In addition to the sumptuous noontime meal which Mother had prepared, we feasted on the latest gospel songs. It was a real cacophony of sound, the songs impressing us by their rhythm and harmony, which were always more interesting than the text.

I am reminded that all of the family's music started out in shape-note form. When, during the course of our career, we added secular music, we depended upon our pianist and mentor, Larry Walker, to acquaint us with the melody. The harmonies then magically fell into place, with only the lyrics of the song before us.

Recently my brother, Bob, found a green file box, in which were stashed away the lyrics of many secular songs. When I took out the "A" folder, for example, I found typed on pieces of paper only the words to "Alexander's Ragtime Band," "I'm Alabamy Bound," "Always," "Ain't We Got Fun"—no music! At the edge of these lyrics, Mr. Walker had penciled in "C-G7," "A" or some other key notation.

When I ran across the lyrics of "And Then It's Heaven," I saw where my father had printed shape notes under the text. I suppose he wanted to make certain he sang his bass part correctly! Shape notes always provided that kind of singing security.

In the 1930s publishers of church hymnals offered either round- or shape-note editions. I do not recall ever singing a gospel song in round notes. Whereas round-note hymnals were generally found in cities and towns (in what were considered more "formal" churches), in the rural areas where we sang, shape notes were used almost exclusively. Occasionally, one discovered a church which used a primary hymnal with round notes and a supplementary paperback one with shape notes.

My mother must have been impressed with Dad's recently acquired knowledge of music, because she purchased on credit a new Gibson guitar and they started singing duets. We children listened to them and became acquainted with some of their music. Soon we were all captivated by the gospel songs which Dad had brought with him from Texas.

When I was in the early grades, I had an after-school job at the Midget Food Store up the street. I kept an inventory of the bag supply and became known as the "little midget egg seller"! On Saturdays I was particularly busy, which meant missing some of Dad's music lessons. Eventually I learned the different shapes of notes and could sing some of the simple exercises. Dad used a pointer on the chart to indicate the difference between 4/4 or march time and 3/4 or waltz time. Likewise with the rests. We counted simple exercises.

Mother and Dad loved to sing the popular songs of the 1920s, but with the children they switched to gospel songs out of the Stamps-Baxter/Vaughan music tradition. The Stamps brothers published their songbooks in Dallas, Texas, which was also the site of their summer music school. James D. Vaughan was in Lawrenceburg, Tennessee, and printed his songbooks there. Another well-known singing family—the Speer Family—began in Lawrenceburg. We were happy to meet the Speers when we attended the summer music school there in June of 1940.

Our family felt fortunate to be able to attend in successive years the music schools of the leading gospel song publishers of the day—the Vaughan School of Music in Lawrenceburg, Tennessee, in the summer of 1940, and the Stamps-Baxter School of Music in Dallas, Texas, in the summer of 1941. We left both Dallas and Lawrenceburg with boxes of the latest songbooks, with several songs added to our repertoire, and with great enthusiasm for our music career.

Quartet music in the 1930s emphasized close harmony, similar to barbershop quartet music, and sometimes gospel songbooks included selections more secular in nature. Composer Albert E. Brumley was a family favorite; his "There's a Little Pine Log Cabin" became something of a signature song for the family and was one of our early recordings for Columbia Records.

Gospel song lyrics were laden with escapist theology, which emphasized the rewards of heaven. What the spiritual was to blacks during American slavery, the gospel song was to the poverty-stricken hordes of the Depression, especially in the South.

As late as 1938, millions of people were unemployed despite the best efforts of Roosevelt and his New Deal programs. Survival was easier for those who could sing their troubles away, dreaming about heaven and the rewards of clean living!

Thus music became an emotional outlet for millions, including my family. As we tried to banish our troubles with singing, we discovered a remarkable blend of voices and an authentic sound growing out of our condition of near poverty. We could sing from the heart, because the message came from experience.

On a warm fall afternoon in 1938, when I was ten years old and had just entered the fourth grade, I climbed onto the rooftop of the apartment complex and walked across to the edge of the corner section. As I mounted the ledge, I saw one of the most glorious sunsets I had ever seen. I sat there enthralled by the beauty and warm glow of the day's ending, feeling good that my family was finally together. I had heard my parents talk about our singing as a family and our possible move from Greensboro. Both ideas excited me. I was especially intrigued with the idea of living in the country with trees and flowers and fields and wide-open spaces. I had had my fill of apartment living, especially after that devastating tornado.

As dusk began to fall, I visualized my family standing up and singing in churches and other places. When our family started performing together, Betty sang the lead; Mother, alto; Dad, bass; and I sang baritone. The twins, Bob and Jim, doubled with Mother or Dad. Singing together as a family gave me a feeling of security and indescribable joy. The future seemed as beautiful as the sunset! It was, indeed, a move beyond the "dirty dishes" and an omen of things to come.

In the winter of 1938, Dad secured another weaving job, this time in the community of Glen Raven, near Burlington. One of the workers there had told him about a farmer named Jim Tickle who owned a cabin that was available for rent. After visiting Mr. Tickle, Dad rented the cabin for eight dollars a month.

Our apartment belongings were loaded onto a truck, and, on March 25, 1939, we moved to the Tickle cabin, located on a long hill in the middle of a group of tall pines. We really were "tickled" to be there! The cabin, which had only two large rooms and a small kitchen at the back, was no larger than the apartment, but the surroundings were spacious. This house also gave us a sense of privacy and provided us with a setting for one of our most popular songs, "There's a Little Pine Log Cabin," which we would later record for Columbia Records. The cabin inspired other songs which would become part of our repertoire. We had no running water, but we did have a marvelous spring at the bottom of the hill, where Mother kept butter and milk and other perishables. In the summer months, nothing was more refreshing than a dipper of cold water from that spring.

We now laugh about our Sears and Roebuck catalogue, which we scanned with interest and which was later used in the outdoor john! We all were embarrassed one day when a heavy windstorm scattered the pages across the hillside. We then boarded up the perimeter walls of the privy, making sure this wouldn't happen again.

Mother worked briefly at a nearby silk mill. Gradually quartets came to visit us, especially on Saturdays, when Dad would lead them in a lesson from the music chart. I learned his spiel myself, becoming his assistant. In addition, invitations started arriving from nearby churches for services, homecomings, and reunions. Singing schools were also added to the agenda.

We never advertised our services. People found out about us by word of mouth. Dad and I usually held singing schools in rural churches. People would gather before Dad's music chart and he would teach them, just as he had taught us family members. On occasion, he would call on me to assist him with the chart or do some of the note singing myself.

The last part of the evening session consisted of what today would be called a vocal jam session. Copies of the latest gospel songbook would be passed out and the people would be asked to turn to one of the easier selections and begin to sing their particular part by note. There would be chuckles and smiles all over the place as hard-working farmers lustily sang their first line of notes! In retrospect, I would have to say the singing schools were as much social as they were educational.

We ordered the songbooks on consignment, paying for them after they were sold. As special representatives of the company, we could get them at a 20–25 percent discount. If one ordered the songbooks individually, one had to pay the list price. For example, *Wings of Love* (Maryville, Tennessee: The Hall Music Company, 1941), sold for 35 cents per copy, $3.60 per dozen, and $22.00 per hundred, postpaid.

Singing schools were a prime source of family income during those early days. Printed pictures of the family were also sold. Mother would see to it that we were all dressed up in clean clothes. Dad would pay some local photographer to come out and make our picture. When it was developed, he took it to a local printer who reproduced it on heavy stock paper or cardboard. The picture, which had cost us two or three cents to produce, was then sold for a dime!

Of special interest to my brothers and me were the possum hunting and muskrat trapping between our cabin and the nearby Haw River. Dad and I would place barrels alongside the edge of the river and stretch a wire across the barrel, wrapping a carrot at the center. We would then fill the barrel with six to eight inches of water. The muskrat would sniff the carrot, lean over for it, and fall into the barrel. Even though this animal is a river creature, it cannot swim indefinitely. So it would drown at the bottom of the barrel.

We also did more conventional trapping, using steel traps to snare an unsuspecting muskrat or mink. Back at the cabin, we skinned the animals and stretched their hides out on wire holders to dry. After the pelts were cured, we packaged them for shipment to a fur company in Chicago. During the winter of 1939–1940, Dad and I made several extra dollars from this enterprise.

Mr. Tickle introduced us to tobacco farming. I later learned that we have two kinds of tobacco in North Carolina. In the Piedmont we have the flue-cured variety and, in the mountains, the burley or air-cured variety. Mr. Tickle, of course, taught us how to grow the flue-cured kind. Before harvesting began, we went through the rows of tobacco and stopped at each plant to remove the small branches between the tobacco stalk and leaf; this process is called suckering. In the summer of 1939, we all pitched in to help Mr. Tickle with the suckering. If this were not done, it would cause the tobacco leaf to drop off.

I remember going through the rows of tobacco with a mule and sled, loading up the tobacco leaves and taking them to a nearby barn, where they were strung on small poles and then hung in the loft of the barn for curing. In those days, wood fires were used to produce heat, which circulated over and around the poles of tobacco. After the curing was completed, the leaves were removed from the poles, placed in a stack, tied in a sheet, put on a truck, and taken for auction to a nearby tobacco market.

Unfortunately my father became addicted to tobacco at an early age and smoked until his death in 1989. When I visited him in the hospital after his heart attack, he proudly announced, "Son, I've quit smoking!" I smiled, replying, "I know, Dad. You've quit smoking because they don't allow it in the hospital." He then confessed, "You're right . . . when I get out I may get me a little chew when I leave the building!" He died a week later.

I remember that, on the Tickle farm, one of the twins experimented with some chewing—only to find himself experiencing what he thought was a fatal illness!

Some of us joined Mr. Tickle in guarding his roadside watermelon patch. At night we would set up our sentinel in a small tent at the back of the patch. We would then await the stealers, who would park their cars or trucks just over the knoll and sneak into the patch. We would monitor their stealthy movements by moonlight, and as soon as they had watermelon in hand, Mr. Tickle would turn his 12-gauge shotgun skyward and shoot, which would result in melons being dropped and stealers making a quick retreat to their cars.

We found country life much more pleasant than city life. We didn't mind the close quarters of the cabin because of the other benefits. The worst incident occurred during a thunderstorm, when the lightning struck a big poplar tree near the front door. If it had fallen in our direction, it could have flattened the house and maybe killed some of us. Fortunately, it fell away from the house and was later sawed up, split, and used as firewood.

On the Fourth of July, 1939, we celebrated Independence Day by singing for the Reynolds reunion at a church south of Greensboro. The impression we made must have been positive, for within a few days we received the following letter from a U. S. senator:

July 10, 1939

The Johnson Family
R. F. D. 4
Burlington, N. C.

My dear Friends:

I was very happy indeed to have been provided the opportunity of attending the Reynolds reunion on July 4 at which time one of your youngsters, one of the little boys with a white suit on, introduced himself to me and presented me with one of your cards.

Was exceedingly regretful that I could not remain after the delivery of my address pertaining to my five point Americanization program. This was due to the fact that I had to speak over Station WBIG at Greensboro and was occasioned to leave immediately after my address, as aforesaid.

With assurances of my best wishes for all the members of the Johnson family, I am,

Very sincerely yours,
(Signed)
Robert R. Reynolds, U. S. S.

Dad had brought not only inspiration with him from Texas but some nicknames as well. Because of some character whom he had met and liked in Dallas, I became "Bugger Red." Since my hair was red, this was later shortened to "Red." Jesse and Lydia became "Pa" and "Ma" Johnson.

Among the unusual experiences of our single year in Burlington was a Christmas visit to Dad's mother near Denver, North Carolina. Shortly before moving from the Greensboro apartment to the log cabin, Dad had made a surprise visit to see his mother and half-sisters, Elizabeth (Lib) and Frances. Not having met him before, they thought at first that he was some distant relative on the maternal side of the family. In a conversation, Lib commented, "We wish we had a brother," to which Dad responded, "You do have . . . I am your brother!" He then went on to explain to his sisters how "Granny" Johnson had reared him from birth, separating him from his biological mother. Minnie became quite upset when she learned that Dad had revealed his true identity to the sisters.

My paternal grandmother had married the son of an English immigrant two years after my father was born. Fred Shellem never owned a house during his lifetime, but he was a conscientious gardener. He became the father of two daughters and did what he could to help them through school. After high school, Frances pursued a bookkeeping course at Brevard College but had to drop out before graduation because of insufficient funds. Lib first tried nursing but then switched to a secretarial course.

During our Christmas visit in 1939, I could tell that Dad's mother had not expected us. To accommodate us, she had to make sleeping arrangements with some of her neighbors. We kids found it awkward calling her "Grandmother," yet she tried to make us feel comfortable. Dad was obviously proud of his wife and four children, and I suspect that it was his desire to display some family success that had brought about this first meeting with our paternal grandmother.

After returning to the log cabin and making a subsequent visit to Providence Baptist Church, near Yanceyville, we moved again on February 24, 1940. After the Providence service, a young couple named Ben and Beulah Eason invited us to Sunday dinner at their home in Danville, Virginia. We lingered there for the afternoon, during which time Beulah showed Mother some of her dresses and offered to give her a pretty blue one with a white streamer and bow tie down the back. Mother accepted it gladly and wore it to the Easons' church that night.

At Third Avenue Christian Church in Danville, we met a warm and compassionate minister named M. T. Sorrell, the longtime pastor there who was not only leading his congregation in a magnificent way but who also established Faith Home for Children, now a rehabilitation center, north of Danville. The people welcomed us gladly. The family was so well received that Dad decided we should move there. Brother Sorrell found us a house and asked the church to "pound" us, which meant providing us with a large supply of canned goods. In addition, he took up one or two "love offerings" to help us with the expense of moving. Because of this generosity, we moved to Danville. Were we seeking survival or loving acceptance? I suspect both.

To supplement the meager family income, Dad secured a part-time job as an appliance salesman at a local store. He was always one who could sell refrigerators to Eskimos, even though Kelvinators were not moving so swiftly at the time in

Danville! Two things happened to us in Danville that would alter our singing activities for years to come.

The first experience came in June of 1940 when we took off, on faith, to the Vaughan Music School in Lawrenceburg, Tennessee. In that small midstate town, James D. Vaughan, who still wore a wing-tipped collar, had started a publishing business in 1905 and a school of music in 1911. Interestingly, he had also secured a radio station license for WOAN in Lawrenceburg in 1922, later selling his license to WSM in Nashville. A founding father of the Church of the Nazarene, he was well known for his entrepreneurship, especially in the field of gospel quartet music.

In Lawrenceburg we met the Speers, another family of singers. Young Ben Speer immediately "fell in love" with my sister, Betty. His older brother, Brock, and his sisters, Rosa Nell and Mary Tom, were most kind to us. "Mom" and "Pop" Speer also encouraged us with our singing. When the school ended, we left Lawrenceburg as representatives of the Vaughan Music Company, carrying with us a carload of songbooks we planned to sell on our way back home. We met the consignment agreement eventually; meanwhile, those books became bread and butter for us whenever we could find a hearing!

I remember stopping in Cookeville, Tennessee, where we sang at the local radio station. Betty remembers meeting a wonderful black family there, who gave her a porcelain basket which she has to this day. We traveled the southern route back to North Carolina, driving over many crooked roads and going through mining towns in the bottom part of the Great Smoky Mountain range. One experience especially stands out—our Wednesday-night stop at a white-framed church next to Shooting Creek, North Carolina.

Only a handful of people were present for the prayer meeting. Dad introduced us and explained that we had been to the Vaughan School of Music and would be glad to sing them a couple of songs, if they were interested. Naturally he was not expecting them to turn down a family that appeared so willing! We sang, and afterwards Dad told the group that we happened to have a few books containing the songs we had sung. We sold them for fifty cents apiece. Pictures of the family were also available for only fifteen cents.

"After our next song," Dad told the interested group, "I'd like for somebody with a couple of extra beds to invite us home for the night!" Sure enough, some fellow stepped forward after the service and invited us to his place, provided we could make it up the mountain to his home. He even volunteered to ride the running board as we drove up the hill, so he could fix the small wood bridges that had been washed out by rain! The next morning, the woman of the house prepared us a delicious breakfast with country ham, eggs, grits, and jelly. We thanked them profusely, sang a song, and loaded up for our trip back to Danville.

Shortly after getting home from Tennessee, we had another singing engagement in Gaffney, South Carolina. A trio of singers was riding with us—nine people in all—when an insurance salesman came barreling through a stoplight and hit us in the front, tearing up the right fender. He settled the accident within a couple of hours and wrote us a check for the damages. With that sixty-five dollars in hand, we later removed the damaged fender and spent the money moving our belongings back to Lincoln County, North Carolina—on August 28, 1940—just in time for the four of us children to enroll in school at Northbrook #3 (when Dad enrolled us, he listed his occupation as "music teacher").

We had been in the community of Vale, singing at a homecoming service, when Dad inquired about a vacant house. Someone told him that the Tom Bass house near Reep's Grove Methodist Church was available. We went to see Dan and Nannie Rhyne, who had recently moved from the Bass homeplace to a new house which they had built just down the road. They agreed to rent the two-story dwelling to us for only ten dollars a month.

Soon after moving into the Bass homeplace, near Cat's Square—now the center of an important apple-growing region in west Lincoln County—we appeared at a singing convention in the old Armory Auditorium in Charlotte. The family was a big hit there, especially during that part of the program which was broadcast over the CBS network. Among our newfound friends from that September 30, 1940, appearance were members of the Rangers Quartet, then a very popular group on WBT in Charlotte. With their encouragement and assistance, we were invited to sing on *Grady Cole's Sunday Morning Farm Club*, broadcast from seven to nine.

Well I remember our first regular broadcast over WBT on Sunday morning, December 29, 1940. Mother got the family up at four a. m. to dress for the program. We left home at five and by six had arrived in Charlotte, where we had breakfast at the Brown Derby Cafe on East Morehead Street. Two friendly Greeks there warmed donuts on their grill and poured us coffee—a delectable Sunday morning breakfast for six hungry singers. This became a regular routine on Sunday morning for many months.

Forty minutes later, we parked at the Wilder Building on South Tryon Street for our first regular broadcast. We made our way up on the elevator to the sixth-floor studios of WBT. We were elated about the fact that we were now part of a weekly program over a fifty-thousand-watt, clear-channel station with a sizable listening audience. Before long, fan mail would start to pour in, full of praise for our performances.

The large studio was located directly across the hallway in front of the elevator. Between the studio and the hallway, a small soundproof room housed an assortment of transcriptions with a sixteen-inch turntable. On the other side of the studio was the master control room, containing a large panel of switches and buttons. We could also see, to our right, a small studio accommodating a single announcer.

In the main studio where we sang were a piano, organ, desk, and assortment of microphones and music stands. Two or three rows of chairs for spectators were set up between the transcription room and broadcast area. If I were to walk blindfolded into that room today, I believe I could go unassisted to the microphone into which we sang for over a decade, a time during which we also did recording sessions for Columbia Records.

A much larger studio was located on the ground floor of the old Wilder Building. That studio had an elevated stage area and could accommodate a greater number of singers and musicians; also, more people could be seated in the audience area. In this studio we did the *Carolina Calling* network program, which included all of the staff singers and musicians: the Briarhoppers, the Rangers Quartet, the Johnson Family, and others.

Dad worked out a special eating arrangement for our second broadcast in Charlotte. He talked his Greek friends at the Brown Derby into providing us with donuts and coffee in exchange for wild rabbits which he had shot or trapped. Inasmuch as we were paid only ten dollars weekly for our performances by the station, this was a useful and satisfactory solution to our need for a morning meal. Going for our Sunday breakfast at the Brown Derby was a great treat for us youngsters, one to which we eagerly looked forward each week.

When the summer of 1941 arrived, Dad arranged for us to embark upon our most ambitious trip to date—a trailer trip to the Stamps-Baxter School of Music in Dallas, Texas. A fellow near Maiden who liked our singing offered to build the trailer for a mere eighty dollars. Bunks were attached to three sides, and a fold-out table provided a place where we could eat. There was plenty of storage space under the bunks. Clothes were hung on a rod down the center of the trailer. It was nothing fancy; however, with a lantern and flashlight and outdoor stove, we were ready for travel.

Our first stop was by the Tennessee River, near Newport, Tennessee, where we camped on a dirt road and fished beside the trailer on the riverbanks. When people living in the area heard about us, they came by, inviting us to visit in their homes, where we would inevitably end up singing. It was a pleasurable if not a lucrative part of the trip.

In Chattanooga we were given a sack of potatoes and a fresh ham, which we tried to keep cool with chunks of ice when we were on the road and in storage underneath the trailer when we stopped. (The ham made it to Dallas, but one day we had left it under the trailer, and, when we returned, the scattered papers told the story. Some hungry dog had discovered it while we were away!)

Among the other singing groups which we met while passing through Arkansas to Dallas was the Humbard Family. A lead singer in this family group was Rex Humbard, who would later become a well-known Ohio pastor and television evangelist. During this early period of our career, another evangelist—J. Harold Smith—wanted us to join him in his tent revivals in Kentucky, but we turned him down.

One of our stops included Terrell, Texas, where Dad proudly introduced us to the man who had been his benefactor on his first trip to the Dallas school—the funeral home director. He was pleased to meet us and seemed proud of the "investment" he had made in Dad.

Whenever money would get low, my father had an interesting way of "earning" handouts for the family. We would pull up to a service station or country store while we were singing. When the attendant came out to wait on us, we would finish the song before telling him what we wanted. He would often invite us in to sing for others. During those store visits, we children would get a soft drink or candy bar or something else to eat. After the car was serviced, the proprietor and others would be so grateful for the music that they would often decline any payment. Thus, we often literally sang for our supper!

On our return from Texas, we were within three miles of home when the axle on the trailer broke. We were also broke financially! I remember Mother counting less than two dollars in her pocketbook. Only a "Pa" Johnson could have led his growing family into such risky ventures with no financial backing. Dad was undoubtedly one of the original possibility thinkers!

Dan and Nannie Rhyne raised eight acres of cotton. We were hired to help them at harvest time. Their sons, Don and Hayden, became our friends and we would often pick in the fields together, throwing cotton bolls at each other. My mother was the champion picker, always exceeding two hundred pounds in the weigh-in of her cotton.

Because of fan mail and other correspondence, Dad purchased a small

Smith-Corona typewriter for me and I became the family secretary. I set up an "office" in the middle upstairs room, where we nailed together some boards with cubbyholes for the different letters.

While I was a conscientious secretary, I was also very much a boy, as was proven when Dad took me to Reinhardt's Barbershop at Henry, past Thern and Eva Sain's store. There Dad and the twins got regular haircuts. When Mr. Reinhardt asked me how I wanted mine cut, I told him to take it all off! With Dad's approval, he proceeded to do precisely that. When I returned home baldheaded and Betty saw me, she burst into tears, ran to her room, and declared she would never sing with me again.

When fall came, we took special delight in going to the different corn shuckings in the community. A farmer would invite neighbors in to shuck his corn, after which there would be plenty of good food to eat. For a growing adolescent, this was also a good time to flirt with the girls and see them smile back at the boys. Those were the times when I felt that God wanted me to be a farmer instead of a singer!

Dad and I taught singing schools over the western end of Lincoln County—at Reep's Grove, Zion, Trinity, Macedonia, and Hebron churches, to name a few. To these churches we would always bring the ever-present music chart and a supply of songbooks. People would sing and enjoy themselves even if they didn't learn much music!

While my father had many different jobs during his lifetime, I never expected him to qualify as a public school music teacher. For one thing, he lacked education credentials, which were necessary for certification. He would delight in telling people he had been through Elon when they asked, "Which was your college?" It was true that we often passed through Elon College, a small town between Greensboro and Burlington! Because of his popularity and personality he was hired, though, by the Lincoln County school system. I remember traveling with him on one occasion to teach a class at the Iron Station Elementary School, where the children sang lustily.

The distance between Lincoln County and WBT seemed to be getting farther and farther as the months passed by. We went about our singing for homecomings and other appearances in the usual manner, but we also started inquiring about a house closer to Charlotte. In the fall of 1941, luck came our way with the location of a log dwelling in east Lincoln County, just off Highway 16 at a place called Triangle. While this cut our driving time in half, the house was much older than the Bass house near Cat's Square.

The Sunday before we moved, Dad drove us over to Rob Graham's to look at the house and to make arrangements for moving in, which we did the following week. His wife, Cordie, an uncommonly well-dressed woman, invited us into their home. In came Dad and Mother and the children and guitar! Within a few minutes we were standing in the hallway, singing for the older Grahams and their children, Ben, Mary, and Margaret. That song cinched the move to Triangle on November 26, 1941!

Mr. Graham's great-grandfather, General Joseph Graham—a soldier in the American Revolution—had moved to Lincoln County in 1792. His son, John D. Graham, later inherited a thousand acres from his soldier-father. In 1822 he started constructing a magnificent brick home, which he named Elmwood and which overlooked the Catawba River. Built by English carpenters and some slave labor, it took five years to complete. At about the same time, John Graham built another house of far less grand proportions a quarter-mile away. That was the log structure which was to become the home of the Johnson Family Singers.

The Graham history has other interesting sidelights. One of John Graham's sons, Robert Clay Graham, eventually inherited the thousand acres; when he died, the land went to the six Graham children. Johnny and Rob were two of these children, and the house we lived in—located on a dirt road that led off from another dirt road—was located between their houses. Their eldest sister, Mrs. Oscar Long, inherited the land containing the homeplace, Elmwood. Like her brothers Rob and Johnny, Jenny Long also reared eight children. Unfortunately, the filling of Lake Norman as a water reservoir for the Duke Power Company twenty years after our move to Charlotte inundated both Elmwood and our cabin.

Years before our move to the Rob Graham cabin, the logs had been boarded up, which helped with the insulation. A bountiful supply of wood and an efficient potbellied stove kept us warm. One Sunday morning in early December, Dad took my brothers and me to search out a nearby creek for possum and coon tracks. When the stream became too large for tracking, we walked the banks. We discovered that we were just below Elmwood, so we went up the hill to visit Oscar and Jenny Long. To our surprise, we found them with their ears glued to the radio, listening to reports of the Japanese bombing of Pearl Harbor. Their son, William, who was with his parents on the morning that President Roosevelt would later call "a day of infamy," was drafted into service a few months later and lost his life in France on November 16, 1944.

We children became especially fond of Kathryn Graham, Johnny and Ethel's youngest child and only daughter. We are still friends, after all these years. My sister and Kathryn were the same age and shared the same interests, including boys! "Aunt" Ethel's peach pie was a favorite. Mother once made twin corduroy jackets for Betty and Kathryn. On some occasions, the Graham daughter would go with us to our Sunday morning broadcast, which later resumed over WBT. Her brothers—all seven of them—were in service during World War II, and each one returned home safely after the war.

Our weekly ten-dollar paycheck from WBT stopped arriving in the spring of 1942. For some unknown reason, WBT discontinued our services on Sunday morning. I suspect the layoff happened not because of our singing but because of the absence of a sponsor. Times became difficult for the family. The tempo of homecomings, singing schools, and farm work had to be stepped up. Oscar and his son, Fred, hired me to plow corn in the river bottoms. Since I was in school, I worked on Saturdays, following a mule from sunup to sundown for a whopping three dollars!

Rob and Carl Nixon supplied us with credit for food at their Triangle stores. Russell Cherry, who operated a store down Highway 16, also helped us through the lean days of summer. For a few weeks, Dad again found mill work across the Catawba River in Cornelius. During the summer of 1942, he and I both worked on a wheat-threshing machine.

Two other people I remember fondly were Clarence and Essie Proctor, neighboring farmers the same age as my parents. Clarence liked to join Dad and me in a review of the latest songbooks from Vaughan and Stamps-Baxter. Since we were all wedded to shape notes, we would often go over songs when the new books arrived, singing only the names of the notes. Harmonizing with syncopated rhythms was quite a challenge.

My educational goal had been to quit school after the eighth grade and work with Mother and Dad in the music business. A trip with Rob Graham to Davidson College, though, changed all that. Mr. Graham made weekly visits to the college across the river, selling butter and eggs. Since I didn't have anything more exciting to do, I often joined him. Several of the professors and President Walter Lingle were his customers.

When I saw the attractive buildings of the Davidson campus, the thought of attending there interested me, and I rejected the plan to quit school after the eighth grade. Later, during the height of our singing career, I did indeed enroll at Davidson and proudly graduated from that institution in 1952. (I was originally to be in the class of 1951, but I had to drop out a year to help with family business.) Rob Graham, I am confident, never was aware of the consequence of my joining him on his egg-and-butter trips to Davidson. It was an important turning point in my life.

The 1942 Rose Bowl game was played in Durham, North Carolina, having been switched from Pasadena because of the war. We listened to the game over Johnny and Ethel's living room radio and were sad to hear Duke lose 20 to 16 to Oregon State. (Little did I realize on that New Year's Day that I would later receive my Master of Divinity degree from Duke.) Today's home entertainment center consists of stereos, AM-FM radio, cassettes, CDs, and television, usually located in the living room or family room, and it is not unusual for additional television sets to be found in the bedrooms. Not so in the days of that Rose Bowl game! Most homes then had only an AM radio, usually kept in the living room, and, often, a 78 rpm record player in another part of the room. That was it . . . no tapes, no videos, no VCRs!

Due to the slowdown of programs in our fledgling radio career, Dad came up with yet another of his creative survival techniques. By trapping rabbits, which we would sell for fifty cents, we could buy gas for our trips to Charlotte. He even tried raising turkeys, but we were not as lucky with them. Dad had bought a few turkey chicks and kept them in the children's quarters in the large upstairs loft, where we had to tolerate their incessant peeps as best as we could. Fate intervened. One night they escaped their meshed-wire pen and fell innocently into the cracks of the wall! We had a hard time enduring their death peeps but decided their entombment was better than removing the boards.

Thanks to help from the Rangers Quartet, we were reemployed by WBT. The Rangers had encouraged management to hire us back for the Sunday morning program with Grady Cole, resulting in another move on November 13, 1942, which took us to the outskirts of Charlotte. As usual, the method of finding a rental house was to inquire at a country store. This time the store was located at McClure's Circle, just off Highway 16. The house, belonging to one of the McClures, was next to "Uncle Andy's" old house. A bachelor, Uncle Andy became a real friend and neighbor.

The road in front of the old Pleasant Grove Methodist Church is now called Pleasant Grove Road, but in the early days it was called Possum Walk. Across the road from the church and down three or four hundred yards in the edge of the woods was another house that had never been painted. We seemed destined to live in log houses without paint! This became our home for the next three years, even though it lacked running water and indoor plumbing. Not until we were juniors in high school did we have that luxury.

Our roots were down for the first time in the Oakdale section of Mecklenburg County, which in subsequent years became part of the city of Charlotte. No longer were we vagabonds of song. In the Queen City we became integrated into the life of a church and community.

Once again we were regular performers at WBT, a position which would continue until 1951. During the next decade, our lives revolved around a studio clock! That decade also saw us children grow up, graduate from high school, and begin our college careers. All of this happened as the Johnson Family Singers flourished on radio and recordings.

THE STUDIO CLOCK

The studio clock. Bulova. Twelve inches in diameter; black arms on a white background; large red second hand. It stood on the wall between our microphone and the master control room.

When we appeared for our first WBT program on December 30, 1940, the studio clock was there, and it continued to be an important presence in our lives through the final program in May of 1951. If we needed to prolong a song to fill out a program segment, I would hold out both hands in a stretching manner; if the song needed to be shortened, my index finger would cross my neck, and we would stop at the first opportunity. These hand signals helped us adjust to the filling of a ten-minute, fifteen-minute, or thirty-minute time slot.

Timing was everything! During our growing years, we felt that we were the most scheduled children that ever lived, and we envied the comparative leisure of other children. My brothers, Bob and Jim, still resent the fact that they were deprived of a normal childhood. When we weren't working on a radio program or engaged in a recording session, we were traveling to an appearance somewhere. We had no time to get into trouble. (The clock's influence has persevered throughout my life. To this day, I try to keep appointments on time, and, over a forty-three-year span in pastoral ministry, I have seldom kept the congregation past the noon hour. In fact, one of my thoughtful parishioners observed that my preaching speeded up if a glance at my watch indicated we might be going past twelve o'clock!)

Before looking at the programs and personalities of those golden days of radio, let me make some general observations.

Radio programs usually started with a theme song. For example, one theme written by Larry Walker went like this:

> When the family gets together 'round the old log cabin,
>> the sound of voices singing fills the air;
> When they start to harmonizing 'round the old log cabin,
>> you'll never find a worry or a care.
> Ma, Pa, Betty, Red, Jim and Bob—
>> with music and happiness to share.
> When the family gets together 'round the old log cabin,
>> that's when I want to be there.

Also important was the personality of the announcer. WBT was blessed with a cluster of excellent announcers. Among those on our programs were Grady Cole, Lee Kirby, Kurt Webster, J. B. Clark, Fletcher Austin, Clyde McLain and Larry Walker, each of whom was a celebrity to our listeners across the Carolinas.

Unfortunately, I kept no diary or log of the various programs across our eleven-year career at WBT, but I have been able to acquire several program transcriptions and scripts, with show names and dates (see Radio Transcriptions). Transcriptions were usually metal, with a vinyl covering on both sides. They were sixteen inches in diameter, which meant they could not be played on a typical player; usually a large studio player was required. During the war years, glass disks were sometimes used, but they were not very durable and were susceptible to breakage.

An orderly listing of our programs is important for several reasons. For one thing, it shows how our music expanded from a repertoire of gospel songs and hymns to a wider variety, including the popular songs of the day. Also, it is possible to trace the developing voices of the children. Never shall I forget the key adjustments which Dad had to make when the voices of the boys started changing. During our adolescence, he had to adjust his faithful capo weekly, or so it seemed!

Our program format was determined by station management; however, the song selections were left to us. Initially Dad decided upon the songs we were to sing, but gradually this responsibility shifted to me.

As the family's music career prospered, our responsibilities grew. I cannot overstate the contribution which Mother made. We children attended school, did homework like other kids, worked at the studio, made records, and traveled to distant places. Mother had the most strenuous schedule of all. In addition to performing on radio and records and appearing before live audiences, she cooked, washed, ironed, sewed, gardened, canned food, and kept the house spic and span.

Every nook and cranny was dusted thoroughly. With all of her mountain of work, she never complained or considered getting any household help. She loved doing it herself.

During the early weeks of 1942, the family had our own WBT broadcast, a "sustaining slot" on Saturday mornings at ten o'clock. We still sang on the *Sunday Morning Farm Club*, from seven to nine, where we had started two years earlier, but gradually we began to branch out into programs of our own. That same year, a man from Florida who was to have a major influence upon our lives joined the station. He was also destined to put Charlotte's first two television stations on the air—WBTV and WSOC-TV—before his retirement in 1962 and his death in 1964. Larry Walker was a smiling, vivacious ex-vaudevillian.

When Larry first came to WBT, he and his wife, Pat, were doing a live radio series for a Florida grocery chain which was fed to stations there. Larry also worked with the Rangers Quartet. By the end of 1943, the Johnsons and Walkers had developed a warm friendship. We also found ourselves being accompanied on the piano by "Uncle Larry."

Until the Walkers arrived, we sang only gospel songs. Larry Walker introduced us to popular music. Shortly after we met him, he was asked by the Charlotte Rotary Club to bring some talent from the station to perform at one of their meetings. When Larry spoke to the station manager, Jess Willard frowned, saying, "Larry, the Johnsons can sing only gospel songs." Larry responded, "Okay, Jess, I'll teach them a popular song!" The night of the Rotary program, the family made such a hit that the men demanded an encore. Knowing only one popular song, we sang it through again!

A native of Manning, South Carolina, Larry was the youngest son in a family of ten children, five sons and five daughters. He was a natural-born musician with perfect pitch; he could be riding along or walking, far away from any instrument, and, when asked to sound a certain key, could give the note instantly. We had never met anyone with this gift.

A winsome and enthusiastic personality, Larry Walker was also the epitome of kindness and patience. I never saw him lose his temper or speak angrily to anyone. Occasionally he would be afflicted with a splitting migraine headache, yet no one could ever tell it by the way he smiled and sang. "Aunt Pat" and "Uncle Larry" quickly became part of our extended family.

Larry's older sister Caro was practicing the piano one day when her youngest brother was only two and one-half years old. As the fifteen-year-old sister played, little Larry kept jumping in his mother's arms. "Get up, Caro, get up!" the mother

Ma Johnson's Craven-Chrisco family portrait, 1913. Lydia Craven (Ma Johnson) is the little girl dressed in white in the center. Lydia's mother, Berta, is third from left; her stepfather, Leroy Chrisco, is fourth from left.

Seaman First Class Jesse Johnson (Pa Johnson), 1922

Lydia (Ma Johnson) on her twenty-seventh birthday, January 21, 1934

Betty and Kenneth Johnson, 1935

Lydia and twins, Bobby and Jimmy, walking up Elm Street,
Greensboro, North Carolina, 1936

Kenneth, "Little Midget Egg Seller," Midget Food
Store, Greensboro, North Carolina, c. 1938

Would You Like to Sing?

Simple method that will benefit any beginner wanting to
learn music. Duets, trios,
quartets, church groups, individuals trained efficiently.

We are representatives of
National Music Co., Fort
Worth, Texas, for song books
with old and new songs.

ORDER FROM

THE JOHNSON FAMILY
R. F. D. 4   BURLINGTON, N. C.

THE JOHNSON FAMILY

Advertisement card for singing school, 1939

DIXIE'S FOREMOST SINGING FAMILY
"THE JOHNSONS"

WOULD YOU LIKE TO SING?

SIMPLE METHOD THAT WILL BENEFIT ANY BEGINNER
WANTING TO LEARN MUSIC. DUETS, TRIOS, QUARTETS,
CHURCH GROUPS, INDIVIDUALS TRAINED EFFICIENTLY

RADIO AND CONCERT SINGERS

ANY TIME ● ANYWHERE

Vaughan School of Music advertisement, summer 1940

The Johnson Family Singers, at "Uncle Andy's" house, Charlotte, North Carolina, 1942

Jim, Bob, Betty, Kenneth ("Red"), Ma, and Pa, "Uncle Andy's" house, 1943

The Johnson Family singing in WBT radio broadcasting studio, Charlotte, 1943

WBT studio photograph, 1943

Red, Ma, Pa, Bob, Jim, Betty, "Uncle Larry" Walker at the grand piano in the studio of WBT radio, Charlotte

Red, Jim, Bob, Ma, Betty, and Pa in their new home in Charlotte, 1946

Pa and Ma, 1947

Red and Betty, 1947

Jim, Bob, Pa, Red, and dog, 1947

Harding High School graduation picture of Betty
and Kenneth, May 1947

Ma and Pa Johnson, WBT studio, 1948

"Uncle Art" Satherly, Red, Bob, Betty, Ma, Pa, Jim, and Don Law

The Johnson Family Singers, Veterans Hospital, Roanoke, Virginia, c. 1949

The Johnson Family Singers at Grandfather Mountain, North Carolina, June 1951. Betty is seated on stage.

"Singing on the Mountain," Grandfather Mountain, 1951

Jim, Bob, Red, Betty, Ma, and Pa going to radio broadcast, 1950

The Johnson Family singing on the Ed Sullivan Show, March 30, 1958: (front) Jim and Ma; (back) Bob, Red, Pa, and Betty

The Johnson twins, Jim and Bob, working as pages for NBC television, New York, in the early 1950s

Betty, c. 1960

Ma and Pa, April 7, 1979 (four days before her death)

finally told the daughter. "I think the baby wants to play!" Whereupon the mother put the little fellow on the piano stool, and he immediately played the same piece his older sister had been practicing!

When the young prodigy was sixteen, his piano teacher told the parents that she had taught him all she could. Larry was then sent to Troy, New York, for special study. Later he graduated from the Comstock Conservatory, during which time he composed music for the Ziegfeld Follies. Meanwhile, the talented musician/arranger had developed friendships and played with such celebrities as George Jessel, Edgar Bergen, Jack Benny, George Burns, and Sophie Tucker.

Larry was the only American student of Jan Paderewski, the great Polish pianist, who once said that Larry had perfect piano hands—each could cover better than an octave and a half! In addition to the four Ziegfeld Follies that Larry staged, he did a classical act for the Keith Circuit, which later became R. K. O. He was introduced to his future wife, Pat, by Irving Berlin. Also included in his New York credits was a radio show for the fledgling CBS network.

At nineteen, Pat went to New York to do a musical show with Oscar Hammerstein II. From New York, she went on the R. K. O. Orpheum Circuit, which took her to Los Angeles. While Pat was on the West Coast, Mr. and Mrs. Edward L. Doheny heard her sing. They invited her to their home and later paid her expenses for two years of study in Milan, Italy. Upon her return to the States, she did a year's concert tour before becoming a commentator and soloist for the Margaret Ann radio series.

Little did I know in those days of work with my family and Pat Walker that, as a United Methodist pastor, I would be called upon to conduct her funeral in Charlotte on September 26, 1983. Earlier, Pat's godchild, Margaret Ann Schwartzburg, hosted a luncheon for family and friends. At the conclusion of the meal, my brother Bob stood and announced to the group, "If I can get my brothers, Jim and Ken, to stand with me, we're going to sing a song in memory of Mrs. Walker." I was amazed that after forty years, the three of us could recall pitch and harmony and lyrics of "Dear Old Girl."

One of Larry's sisters, Julia Bradham Brown (known to us affectionately as "Bumpsy") came to Charlotte with the Walkers in 1942. The youngest of the Bradham girls, she had been widowed by a naval officer the previous year. It was Julia who told me how, early in his music career, Larry had legally changed his name from Laurens Walker Bradham to the shortened Larry Walker. They had a deaf-mute brother who had graduated from Gallaudet College in Washington when Dr. Laurens Walker was president. In appreciation of

Dr. Walker, the Bradhams named their youngest child after him; however, in show business Larry found that the surname caused difficulties with spelling and pronunciation.

In the early part of 1944, Larry moved from accompanying the Rangers Quartet to playing for my family, and he also sang with us, as did his wife on certain occasions. We marveled at the way this classical musician could "tickle the ivories" with all kinds of music! His piano not only complemented Dad's guitar but gave variety to our music. Larry helped us to learn ballads and popular songs, including "Sweetheart of All My Dreams," "Sweet Sue," "Apple-Blossom Time," "When You Wore a Tulip,"and "Rosemary" (see Radio Transcriptions for other songs of the day). Mother's favorite, which she later taught our children, was "On Moonlight Bay."

Dad still had the musical limitations of his mentor, "Wink" Howard. Larry provided us with another dimension to our work, allowing us to be considered a variety-singing group rather than performers of gospel only. Within a relatively short period of time, we had broadened our repertoire in both radio and show appearances. From this time on, we were known as a variety-singing family. But we did not give up the gospel songs and hymns with which we had begun our career and which we considered our bread-and-butter music; we simply incorporated them into a larger body of work.

Among the religious songs which were favorites of our listeners were "In the Shadow of the Cross," "The Old Gospel Ship," "I Feel Like Traveling On," "How Beautiful Heaven Must Be," and "Won't It Be Wonderful There" (again, see Radio Transcriptions for additional songs). Perhaps the all-time favorite was "Precious Memories." When he retired as dean of students at Davidson College, Dr. John C. Bailey, Jr., who was a Greek scholar, wrote me a letter, asking for a copy of this hymn. I was impressed that an erudite man like Dean Bailey would find meaning in such a simple hymn.

On December 15, 1946, the family joined Larry in a guest appearance with the Charlotte Symphony Orchestra in their Christmas concert at the old Armory Auditorium. This was quite a jump in our musicianship from log cabin days!

In addition to our music connection, the Walkers took a personal interest in us and our development, especially my sister and me. When they found that Betty didn't have any heat in her bedroom, they promptly bought a stove for her! We would visit them at their summer cottage in Blowing Rock, with its breathtaking view of the Smokies and the tiny crossroads of Globe down in the valley. Also, we met their friends and would go to parties and other places that they would arrange for us. The social graces to which the Walkers exposed us made us feel more confident as we grew up and widened our circles.

After these many years, I can understand why my mother and brothers were somewhat resentful of the Walkers. Pat and Larry's interest in Betty and me showed an element of favoritism which, in turn, produced jealousy. After all, their dress and refinement were very much in contrast to the family's. While they intended no offense, their having a different cultural background created some feelings of inferiority and resentment.

In defense of the Walkers, I suppose one would have to say that the twins had too much of the prankster in them for anyone to risk out-of-town invitations. Bob, the older twin, confessed to me much later in life that he and Jim would sometimes go into the men's room at WBT, fill paper napkins with water and drop them on unsuspecting people on the street six floors below! On discussing with Mother our relations with the Walkers, she told me that she felt they were simply "using" us. Because of Larry's honesty and sincerity, however, it is my opinion that Mother's assessment was not correct. I believe that, in the absence of any children of their own, Betty and I simply became their child substitutes.

We always felt that the Rangers Quartet liked the family and used their influence to help us join them as staff singers at WBT. Much later on, I learned that brothers Vernon and Arnold Hyles had preceded us at the Stamps-Baxter School in Dallas. They were a gifted twosome. For a brief time at WBT, Vernon Hyles served as program director. Arnold had the lowest bass voice I had ever heard. Walter Leverette was a marvelous baritone, and hearing Denver Crumpler soar into the heights with his clear tenor voice was also a joy.

Some people regarded the Rangers as the best gospel quartet ever. They also had wonderful pianists to accompany them. Marion Snyder was their first, in 1941, and he was succeeded by Charles Friar, Larry Walker, Lee Roy Abernathy, Hovie Lister, Doy Ott, and David Reece. Still later, in the 1950s, Cecil Pollock and Elmer Childress played for them.

There were a few occasions when Walter called me up to fill in for him on some of their radio programs. I felt flattered to be singing with the Rangers Quartet.

Grady Cole was another character I remember fondly. Grady's main interest besides radio was boxing. With his friend Jim Crockett, he helped to promote many matches in the area. It was he who introduced us to Jack Dempsey, one of the most popular heavyweight boxing champions of all time. I later learned that Dempsey was also one of the ring's most fearsome men, with over twenty-five first-round knockouts, more than any fighter in history. The "Manassa Mauler," as sportscasters called him, was visiting Grady one day when we arrived at the station for one of our programs. My little hand felt swallowed up by the huge hand of the heavyweight champion, who had been one of my father's heroes since winning the title over Jess Willard in 1919. Dempsey remained champion until his defeat by Gene Tunney in the fall of 1926.

Grady never related to us as the Walkers did, yet he was the primary announcer for our programs, including the popular Quaker Oats series that closed out our radio career in May 1951. When Grady died in the summer of 1979, I wrote a tribute to him, part of which follows:

> During the 1930s and 1940s, one of the most influential radio men in the Carolinas was Grady Cole, famed announcer at WBT in Charlotte. "His voice sounded like a lawnmower in a gravel pit," wrote Bob Quincy in his *Charlotte Observer* column (7–17–79, p. A–9). The Rev. Glenn Lackey, one of our Methodist preachers, once told me that two mail carriers in his former pastorate at Catawba used to say that they could always tell when Grady had some new sponsor or sales gimmick. Their mail loads would automatically increase!

> "Mr. WBT," as Grady was sometimes called, happened to have been born and died the same year as my mother. But the things I remember most about him relate to my family, who did regular radio shows with him during the forties and early fifties. Homespun in philosophy, Grady Cole's raspy, frolicky voice seemed to me to be a perfect match for the contrasting blend of Johnson vocals. As announcer, disc jockey, farm editor, weather reporter, news commentator and general entertainer, he was incomparable.

> We first met Grady around six-thirty on Sunday morning, December 29, 1940. Why do I remember the exact time? It was my family's first appearance on *Grady Cole's Sunday Farm Club*—a two-hour show that lasted from seven 'til nine. Our singing was interspersed with Grady's comments, humor, farm reports, weather reports, and commercials. We received the grand total of ten dollars for each show—which was supposed to cover our services and expenses from home in the western part of Lincoln County, near a place called Cat's Square!

> Grady was an incessant talker, but a mild and mellow man whose warmth was contagious. He provided a forum for our family and the opportunity for us to develop. Stephen Grellet, the Quaker missionary, once said, "Any good thing that I can do, any kindness that I can show, help me to do it now, for I shall not pass this way again." Grady Cole passed our way and, because of his kindness, we remember him with affection and appreciation.

We remember other people with admiration, including the original Carter Family. For almost a year in the early 1940s, we felt honored to appear on WBT programs with A. P., Sara, and Maybelle, who were later to be included in Nashville's Country Music Hall of Fame. As a youngster, I was fascinated by the twangy, mountain sound of this trio, a group which sang with no animation on their faces but nevertheless produced a sound that was folksy and warm. I was always intrigued by the fact that the Carter Family was in reality an extended family. A. P. and Sara had divorced in the late 1930s but continued singing together, even after Sara had married A. P.'s cousin. Maybelle was another cousin. Their WBT days turned out to be their final working days together.

In addition to these members of the original Carter Family, Maybelle's three daughters—Helen, June, and Anita—had recently started their own musical group. They sang with us on the Grady Cole programs. Although they lived only a few blocks from the radio station, they chose to attend school with us at Paw Creek High School, out in the county. Little did we realize that young June would some day achieve stardom on her own, eventually becoming the wife of Johnny Cash. We were sorry to see Maybelle and her daughters leave WBT for WRVA in Richmond, Virginia.

Another singing group which we admired greatly was the LeFevre Trio of Atlanta, Georgia. We sang at their church in Atlanta and were with them for several appearances. I first became acquainted with the LeFevres in 1942 while we were living in the Graham cabin. Each weekday afternoon around six o'clock, I would turn our little radio dial to Atlanta's WGST, a ten-thousand-watt station that reached into several states, so that I could hear them sing. What a beautiful blend they had! As the station faded, I would put my ear closer to the speaker, not wanting to miss a single note. Urias, Alphus, and Eva Mae were excellent musicians and made an important contribution to gospel music, with their singing as well as their compositions. I felt nostalgic several years later when, at a White House reception, President Jimmy Carter walked across the East Room to embrace his guest and fellow Georgian, Eva Mae LeFevre.

Black singing groups also appeared with us over WBT. The Golden Gate Quartet was a friendly group with whom we sang. On one weekend in the mid-1940s, the famous Wings Over Jordan Choir originated their Sunday network program from the large first-floor studio in the Wilder Building. While black groups were not as numerous as those composed of whites, all of us singers seemed to be color-blind. The early exposure of my sister and brothers and me to black singers and musicians made us feel empathetic to their plight in a segregated society. Consequently, the attitude of racial prejudice that occurred in others did not seem to be a problem for us.

How does one describe the Johnsons during this early period of their radio career? Over the years, many stories appeared in the newspapers, often mixing fiction with fact. For example, on October 17, 1943, the public relations department at WBT placed this ad in the *Charlotte Observer* (section I, p. 2). To me it accurately described the family: "Close harmony that's really close! Ma and Pa Johnson have been singing together since they were courting. And when Red, Betty, and the twins, Bobby and Jimmy, were old enough, they started right in singing, too. The Johnsons are favorites of Southern listeners."

My sister, Betty, was a featured singer on a program called *Briarhopper Time* each weekday afternoon at four-thirty. Before we children started driving, Dad spent his time taking us back and forth between home and school and the radio station. As if our regular shows were not enough, WBT scheduled a "weekly barn dance" program with its top-flight personalities on Thursday nights at eight-thirty; it featured Hank and the Briarhoppers, the Johnson Family Singers, the Rangers Quartet, Whitey and Hogan, Claude Casey, Don White, Shannon Grayson, Fred Kirby, Sam Cantrel and his vibraphone, fiddler George Hefferman, and blues singer Billie Ann Newman.

During the winter of 1943–1944, we did a regular show sponsored by Vick Chemical Company. Our product was "4-way cold tablets" and we appeared on Tuesday, Thursday, and Saturday mornings at 6:45 and Monday, Wednesday, and Friday afternoon at 3:45. Unfortunately, I do not have any transcriptions or scripts of those 4-way cold tablet programs; however, I do have forty-four program scripts and two transcriptions of a weekly CBS program with Larry Walker, which aired in the second half of 1945. The fifteen-minute program came on at 4:45 in the afternoon.

The program for July 25, 1945, provides a glimpse of this series. The theme song was written by Mr. Walker:

Larry: Hello, neighbors!

Family: Hello, neighbors! How is the world treating you?

Larry: If we're to be neighbors,

Family: . . . friendly neighbors,

Larry: Time that we say, "How-de-doo!"

Family (humming), Larry (singing): I came along to make this piano play . . . Help the Johnson Family Singers sing your worries away. Hello, neighbors!

Family: Hello, neighbors! Time to sing . . .

Larry: . . . time to play . . .

All: Time to say "hello" to you!

After completing the theme song with us, Larry continued as announcer:

Hello, everybody, it's time for the Johnson Family Singers, a program of songs by one
of America's outstanding singing families. This is Larry Walker, your musical master of
ceremonies, speaking, and we're all here—Ma, Pa, Betty, Red, and the twin boys, Jim
and Bob, and yours truly—with music on our minds and, well, a song on the tip of our
tongues. As you probably have noticed, we sorta lean toward the old, familiar songs.
And this afternoon, we're startling off with an old favorite of yours that's back again, and
right up among the present-day hits, too. It's the sweet little love ballad "Sweetheart of
All My Dreams."

I remember two moments which were embarrassing to me during our singing
career. One happened toward the beginning of a network program—I have
forgotten which one—when each family member was supposed to introduce
himself or herself. "Hello, friends," my father began. "I'm 'Pa.'" Mother followed,
" . . . and I'm 'Ma.'" My turn came next, so I blurted out unintentionally, "Hello,
Red! I'm everybody!" The family broke up in laughter, with Betty and the twins
finally chiming in to give their names.

The other embarrassment came at a promotional dinner for the Hudepohl
Brewing Company at the Charlotte Hotel, where we were the entertainers. I was
seated across the long table from a brewing company executive. We had steaks
that night, as I recall, and beside each place was a bottle of Hudepohl. As a young
teenager who chose not to drink alcoholic beverages, I asked the executive, "Sir,
how does Hudepohl differ from other beers?" He responded, "I don't see you
drinking any!" The answer to what I thought was polite dinner conversation and
a relevant question made me turn red faced, I'm sure. I remember nothing else
about the evening!

Lee Kirby was our announcer for the cold-tablet programs as well as for
the longer-running BC series from 1947 to 1950. This was a ten-minute Sunday
program, *Hymntime*, at 1:05 p. m.

That program opened with a chord on Dad's guitar, and the family singing the
theme: "Precious memories, how they linger / How they ever flood my soul . . ."

We then hummed the next line, while the announcer said over us, "Good
afternoon, friends, and welcome to *Hymntime*, transcribed with the Johnson

Family Singers, the program of your favorite hymns—old and new—brought to you by the makers of BC headache powers and BC headache tablets. . . ." We then came back in with " . . . Precious, sacred scenes unfold." We always sang three hymns on the program, going into a hum when we ran out of time on the final song.

Lee Kirby was well known to the WBT listening audience for his annual play-by-play description of the Shrine Bowl football game in Charlotte, which pitted the best of football players from North Carolina and South Carolina against each other. He was always immaculately dressed, with a pin-striped tie, and he was blessed with a warm if sometimes raspy voice.

Kurt Webster was another popular announcer, usually associated with a late-night record show on which he played the popular songs of the day. One record which he introduced was "Heartaches" by Ted Weems, which became a number one best-seller. One of our network sustaining shows on CBS with Kurt Webster, August 31, 1947, 8:45 to 9:00 a. m., had the following script:

ANNCR: (COLD) Columbia presents . . . The Johnson Family Singers
MUSIC: THEME (HAVEN OF REST) UP FULL FOR ONE VERSE, CONTINUED HUMMING WITH A FAST FADE FOR:
ANNCR: From deep in the heart of Dixie, Columbia presents the voices of a mother, a father, and their four children . . . known coast-to-coast as The Johnson Family Singers . . . Ma, Pa, Red, Betty and the twins Bobbie and Jimmie. Each week, just before the chimes ring out the hour of worship in the church at the turn of the lane, we invite you to join us in a review of the old hymns and ballads you still love . . . in the sweet, melodic manner of The Johnson Family Singers.
MUSIC: THEME: VOCAL UP FULL TO CONCLUSION:
ANNCR: On this day of rest and meditation, many of us will be thinking of loved ones who have passed on from our family circles. But how can there be sadness when we realize that some bright morning we may join them in eternal joy . . . and share "A Home up in Heaven." The family repeat familiar words with fresh meaning as they sing this inspiring hymn.
MUSIC: A HOME UP IN HEAVEN
ANNCR: Many of our finest hymns are the joyous songs of those souls who have discovered Jesus Christ and His secret to Eternal Life. The family have chosen next a stirring song that is both victorious and eager . . . "Press On, It Won't Be Long!"
MUSIC: PRESS ON, IT WON'T BE LONG

ANNCR: The life that has been wholly given over to God is always a happy, contented one. And one of the most familiar of prayer-songs is the one asking for complete Divine guidance. The family sing the beautiful, "Have Thine Own Way, Lord."

MUSIC: HAVE THINE OWN WAY, LORD

ANNCR: Each week the Johnson Family read carefully the many letters they receive from shut-ins and their friends all over the country. Today . . . as every Sunday . . . they would like to dedicate a special greeting-in-song to the writer of the letter they felt was most deserving. Their appreciation and best wishes go to all of you . . . and to ———— a special song.

MUSIC: (HUMMING) WHERE WE'LL NEVER GROW OLD

ANNCR: I am sure that listeners everywhere would like to send messages of encouragement of their own to ————, whose address is ————. For her/him, the family sings a song of tenderness and faith . . . "Where We'll Never Grow Old."

MUSIC: WHERE WE'LL NEVER GROW OLD . . . UP & FINISH.

ANNCR: The strength and guidance of the Almighty is a powerful necessity for facing the trials of everyday living. So it is only instinctive faith that prompts us to pray . . . "In this world of doubt and gloom . . . When hope's flowers fail to bloom . . . Lord, Lead Me On."

MUSIC: LORD, LEAD ME ON

ANNCR: You will want to remember to send greetings to our shut-in of the week, ———— of ———— and to write the Johnson Family, care of the station to which you are listening, about your shut-in friend . . . or your own story.

MUSIC: (THEME) UP FULL FOR PART-VERSE, CONTINUED HUMMING WITH FAST FADE FOR:

ANNCR: From deep in the heart of Dixie, Columbia has presented the voices of a father, mother and their four children, The Johnson Family Singers . . . in another quarter-hour of songs of the church. This program will be heard at this same time next week, over most of these same stations. Until next Sunday, then, goodbye from the family who wish you a pleasant Sabbath Day and a happy week ahead. This program is written by Patricia Lee and produced by Harry Snook. Kurt Webster speaking. This is CBS, the Columbia Broadcasting System.

Another prominent announcer for the family was J. B. Clark. Tall, debonair, and sporting a neatly trimmed moustache, the deep-voiced Clark loved poetry and used it frequently in our program. Although he was almost mournful sounding, we enjoyed our work with the cigar-smoking J. B.

We received much fan mail, cards and letters alike. Here are two samples:

Dear Folks:

I listen to your program and enjoy it very much. Please sing, "Silver Haired Daddy of Mine" for me. My Dad has been dead a year and send me one of your Christmas gifts. Thanks.

> Mrs. Ernest McManus
> Route 5
> Monroe, N. C.

Dear Johnson Family—

We enjoy listening to your programs so much. Will you please sing, "Lonely River," on your afternoon program some time this week. Will appreciate this very much. My brother, James, likes your programs also. He has been in the Army hospitals for about year and just came home recently. Sorry I did not receive your picture. Wishing you every one a joyous Christmas and a wonderful New Year.

> Sincerely yours,
> Mrs. Annie B. Frieze
> Route # 2
> Mooresville, N. C.

While radio was our main interest, the family also traveled about the Carolinas making appearances at schools, theaters, churches, conventions, singings, and rallies. On one of our singing forays into western North Carolina, Dad inquired about a place where the family could spend the night and was told that The Old Kentucky Home in Asheville took in overnight boarders. At the time I did not know that the place was run by the mother of novelist Thomas Wolfe. In 1994 my brothers and I toured the Thomas Wolfe House (now a state memorial) and learned that the long bed in which Dad and I had slept was earlier used by Wolfe himself. Mother and Betty shared a bed in another room, and the twins slept together in a third. While they couldn't remember the room, Bob and Jim did recall the delicious breakfast prepared by Mrs. Wolfe the next morning. The room and bed in which I had slept looked just the same fifty years later.

One of our long-running sponsors was the BC Remedy Company, and we provided the entertainment for several state pharmaceutical conventions in North Carolina, South Carolina, Virginia, and West Virginia. The most memorable of those was the one held at the famed Green Briar Hotel in White Sulphur Springs, West Virginia. At this convention, Dad and my brothers played a trick on me.

They asked me to call downstairs for room service. When the clerk knocked on the door, they asked me to answer it and place the order. Just before I opened the door, the guys all fell to their knees and started praying audibly! I felt so dumb standing there before a waiter with my brothers and father wailing in the background, "O God, save us! Save our brother and all of the sisters and brothers at this convention . . ." Embarrassed, I apologized to the waiter, telling him that our call to him had been a mistake. When I closed the door, the guys stood up, laughing uproariously. I didn't think it was funny.

Recently while going over some of our files, I saw "show dates" listed in various Carolina cities and towns as well as engagements in other states. Included in my memorabilia for this period is a miscellaneous list of personal appearances.

The thin hard-bound Eureka Family Expense Record has the following index on the inside cover:

1949 Family dates (miscellaneous)	pp. 2–3
Family theater dates	pp. 4–5
1950 Business Entertainment	pp. 6–7
Miscellaneous Dates	pp. 8–9
Personal Expenses of dates	p. 10
1951 Income Tax Information	pp. 14–15
Business Entertainment, Promotion, Deductions, etc.	pp. 18–19

On the top right, I wrote, "The Johnson Family Singers Record Book 1949, 1950, 1951. Kenneth M. Johnson, Secretary."

I have similar records on a photostat from March 12, 1943, to March 26, 1947. To illustrate the information in those records, here is what I wrote down for 1945:

Sun., January 28th Concord, N. C. Westford Methodist Church $30.00
Sun., March 4th Greer, S. C. Victor Baptist Church $40.00
Sat., March 24th Greer, S. C. Victor Grammar School $85.00
Sun., March 25th Greenville, S. C. First Church of God $50.00
Sun., March 25th Greenville, S. C. First Assembly of God $85.05
Sun., March 25th Greer, S. C. Church of God $20.50
Sun., April 1st Mineral Springs, N. C. Pleasant Grove MC $25.27
Tue., April 10th Spruce Pine, N. C. Carolina Theater $94.43
Sat., April 21st Greenville, S. C. Parker High School $150.00
Sun., July 22nd Pageland, S. C. Zion Methodist Church $40.00
Fri., July 27 Cherryville, N. C. home of Blaine Beam $50.00

Sat./Sun., Sept.8–9 Greenville, S. C. Church of God $200.00

Wed., Sept. 12 Charlotte Country Club Bankers Banquet $50.00

Certain duties emerged for different members of the family. Mother, of course, saw to it that we were fed and clothed properly. Like John Wesley, she believed that "cleanliness is next to godliness." Dad helped to arrange for the various programs and engagements. I became closely identified with him in business arrangements for the family.

After moving to Charlotte, Dad opened his first bank account, but arranged for me to sign his name on the checks as well as make the deposits and withdrawals. Regardless of who earned the money, all that we received went through this account. Moreover, I became the "father" in matters of pocket change and allowances!

Betty's role in the family was largely confined to helping Mother with the cooking, clothes, and housekeeping. Bob and Jim did their share of bringing in the wood and helping to keep the place clean. Though our belongings were meager, they always looked good. Combining school with professional work made for an interesting life. We were always anticipating some new show or appearance. Betty was constantly "on stage," and our personality traits were strongly shaped by the public aspect of our lives. Almost on cue, we smiled and became effervescent whenever we walked into classrooms, grocery stores, or social gatherings. Our mentor, Larry Walker, taught us to smile even when we felt miserable.

I ended up helping Larry Walker plan the programs and give hand signals during the broadcasts. As stated earlier, we could adjust numbers, padding or cutting, to meet time requirements with little difficulty by giving the proper signal. Bob doubled with Dad on bass and Jim sang top tenor. If some part were too high or too low for one of us, we'd point to another family member and change parts at the end of a phrase. The listener would never know the difference. For us children, harmony was as natural as melody. Betty's harmonic versatility later appeared in her recordings, where she dubbed the different parts. Mother and Dad were not as keen with their pitch, nor did they pick up new music as well as the children. I always suspected that part of this problem was due to some hearing impairment caused by their mill experiences earlier in life. However, one ability must have been enhanced by their spinning and weaving jobs—they could read lips when uncertain of the lyrics!

Early in the 1940s, still another group came to WBT. We had played some appearances with Arthur Smith and the Crackerjacks while they were still at WSPA in Spartanburg, South Carolina. We welcomed them as regulars to WBT. Brothers Arthur, Ralph, and Sonny were pleasant and easy going. We enjoyed working with them. Later Arthur became the guitarist for our Quaker Oats programs as well as providing fiddle accompaniment for some of our Columbia Records. Sonny joined him at rhythm guitar for one of the record sessions.

Our WBT radio days were filled with associations. Fred Kirby, the son of a Methodist preacher, the Tennessee Ramblers, Whitey and Hogan, Bill Davis, Claude Casey, the Sagedusters, and Elmer "Hank" Warren (also WBT photographer for many years) all were delightful people who made music a fun experience. From their programs and corny jokes, we learned to laugh in the right places!

On October 25–27, 1985, at the Spirit Square Arts Center in Charlotte, the North Carolina Arts Council sponsored a reunion of the Briarhoppers and other entertainers. Dubbed "The Charlotte Country Music Story," it re-created *Briarhopper Time*, which had aired on WBT from 1935 to 1951, and brought together a host of other aging entertainers!

"Y'all know what it is?" said Charles Crutchfield, retired president of Jefferson Pilot Communications, who started out in radio as a WBT announcer in 1933. "It's Briarhopper time!" countered the seven players, greying or balding, who launched into "Wait 'til the Sun Shines Nellie."

"I had forgotten how noisy these boys were," Crutchfield said of Shannon Grayson, Hank Warren, Don White, Claude Casey, Whitey and Hogan (their stage names) and Fred Kirby.

My family reunited with the Briarhoppers. This was our first public appearance since being on the *Mike Douglas Show* in 1965, and our first appearance without Mother, who had died in 1979. On this program, the family sang "Precious Memories." Then Betty, who had become a regular on *Briarhopper Time* at the tender age of fourteen, brought the house down with her rendition of "Red River Valley."

Other well-known artists who appeared on the Spirit Square program included Bill Monroe, legendary "father of bluegrass"; Arthur Smith, known for his recording of "Dueling Banjos"; Snuffy Jenkins, who developed the three-finger picking style characteristic of bluegrass music; Homer "Pappy" Sherrill, who fiddled with many early country music greats including the Blue Sky Boys; the Tennessee Ramblers, with Cecil Campbell, popular string band of the 1930s and featured in motion pictures; Wade Mainer, who with his brother J. E. led the immensely popular and influential Mainer's Mountaineers in the 1930s; and Zeke and Wiley Morris from

Black Mountain, North Carolina, composers of the classic bluegrass song "Let Me Be Your Salty Dog."

Joe and Jannette Carter also participated, paying tribute to the legendary Carter Family. Chapel Hill's popular Red Clay Ramblers were on the program, as was George Hamilton IV.

In addition to our appearance on the re-created *Briarhopper Time*, the family conducted a packed workshop, where Betty led family members in "a stroll down memory lane," recalling many family experiences. In the workshop, Bob accompanied us on the guitar as we sang "There's a Little Pine Log Cabin" and "Where No Cabins Fall." After the second number, Betty looked at me and said, "Brother, you did all right on the lead part in the chorus, but you were not as good as Mother!" I agreed.

One of the questions asked by people in the audience was "How did your school principal work with you in your busy singing schedule?" We answered that our principals and teachers were always cooperative—especially S. A. McDuffie, the principal at Paw Creek. We didn't have to skip many classes, and we always made up any work that we missed.

One person in the audience was curious about our song "The Death of Ellenton," which we recorded for Columbia on May 7, 1951. It probably was one of the first antinuclear songs recorded. Dad wrote it following an emotional outburst by those who were against destroying the town of Ellenton, South Carolina, so that a nuclear power plant could be built there on the Savannah River. This sentiment resonated not only with South Carolinians but with people across the nation.

We discovered at the Spirit Square event that the Library of Congress had included our rendition of "The Death of Ellenton" in its bicentennial program recording, *Songs of Local History & Events*, LBC 12. The booklet accompanying the record, edited by Richard K. Spottswood, carried the text. It also told the story of the atomic energy facility's construction, explaining how every building in Ellenton not relocated was razed, including eight stores, three churches, a paved main street, and a new thirty-thousand-dollar addition to the school which had been completed only a month before the evacuation order. Eight thousand people were displaced. This, indeed, was an event to write and sing about! Mr. Spottswood included a family picture in the story, incorrectly dated 1947 (it was actually made in 1943 or 1944). Because of its historical importance, we have included "The Death of Ellenton" in the CD accompanying this book.

Once when Gene Autry came to town, my brothers and I were hired as back-up singers to augment the music on his Sunday evening program, *Melody Ranch*, over

CBS. That six-thirty appearance proved to be not only musically challenging but also financially helpful, with a large talent check going into the family account for our services. My brother Bob remembers Autry giving each of us a new bicycle as a bonus.

During the war years, we entertained troops at local Morris Field as well as at Laurinburg-Maxton Air Force Base. We even traveled to Fort Dix, New Jersey, for a USO program. On a U. S. treasury war bond program, Betty received an order for a ten-thousand-dollar bond from Mrs. Will McClure. Later we sang at several VA hospitals. Unforgettable also was a CBS show we did that memorialized President Franklin D. Roosevelt after his sudden death at Warm Springs, Georgia. We sang "The Old Rugged Cross" in memory of the only president we children had ever known up until that time! That program was especially impressive to WBT officials.

At the Charlotte Country Music Story program in 1985, Betty told our workshop group how on a visit to London in the 1950s she had met Eleanor Roosevelt on a hotel elevator. After introducing herself to the former First Lady—identifying herself as part of the Johnson Family Singers—Mrs. Roosevelt responded, "O yes, my husband and I used to enjoy listening to your family on the radio!"

When we moved to Charlotte on November 13, 1942, Dad enrolled all of us at Paw Creek High School, about four miles southwest of our home. Excepting those days when Dad took us out for a broadcast or appearance, we rode a bus to school. Although county schools were generally considered inferior to city schools, Paw Creek was noted for its excellence. My brothers remember the traveling minstrel shows which came regularly to our school.

After transferring from Denver High School to Paw Creek, Betty and I were assigned to Clara Pigg's eighth-grade class. To some people, the friendly face of this old maid schoolteacher actually resembled a pig's! She would laugh when telling us that when she died she wanted a male quartet to sing at her funeral "because I've been neglected by men all of my life!"

Several years later, while I was serving a church in Winston-Salem, Miss Pigg died at the nearby Baptist retirement home, where Betty and I had visited her a couple of times. When the local newspaper carried the notice of Miss Pigg's death on May 23, 1971, I wrote my own tribute to this delightful lady for one of our church newsletters. It concludes, "My days at Paw Creek with Clara Pigg seemed far away from where I sat in that funeral service. I kept hoping that some male quartet would appear to sing! In the casket lays the remains of a dear and precious teacher, who gave encouragement to my life."

The principal of Paw Creek High School, S. A. McDuffie—better known to us students as "Mr. Mac"—provided Betty and me with different opportunities to express our musical talent. Inasmuch as the school had no music or drama teacher, Mr. Mac permitted us to stage a musical ourselves during our sophomore year. I even received his permission to organize a choir, which I directed during my final three years of high school. Such were some of the spinoffs of our musical upbringing, which began when a man joined a woman in washing dirty dishes twenty-five years before!

During our junior year at Paw Creek, Betty and I joined Virginia Hauser, Charles Elliott, Ray Plummer and others for a trip to Winston-Salem, where we attended the Beta Club state convention at the old Robert E. Lee Hotel. (We fellows from Paw Creek were the only ones wearing tuxedos for the final banquet!) Since I had been taking piano lessons for about a year, I had mastered one song which I could play while Betty sang. In the talent contest, I accompanied her on "How Deep Is the Ocean" and she won first prize; then, as if that were not enough glory, she and Virginia Hauser and I teamed up as a trio, sang "Juanita" a capella, and won second prize! For some youngsters, confidence is difficult to cultivate; our musical appearances and successes made it easy for us.

Included in our high school experiences was a tour with the Paw Creek High School choir to other county high schools. During the course of our work, I came to know Oliver Cook, choir director at Harding High School in Charlotte. With his encouragement, I attended the vocal camp at Westminster Choir College in Princeton, New Jersey, in the summer of 1945. A year later, we reluctantly left Paw Creek for our senior year at Harry P. Harding High School, where Mr. Cook promptly made me his student assistant.

Looking back over our Paw Creek days, I believe it was the right school at the right time. We would have graduated there, I'm sure, if it had not been for my interest in choral music. After Betty and I graduated from Harding, Bob and Jim returned to Paw Creek for their completion of high school.

Entertainment celebrities make news in most schools. At Harding, as at Paw Creek, people accepted our popularity and seemed proud of the fact that we were there. The December 19, 1946, issue of *Harding Hi-Lites*, the school paper, predicted in a lead story a promising career for their popular senior, Betty Johnson: "How would you like as your Christmas present a $2,000 screen test complete with all the trimmings? That's what Betty Johnson has to look forward to December 22 when she goes to New York at the request and as the guest of Twentieth Century Fox. But that's not all. *Glamour* magazine has also asked her to pose for photographs for use in their publication. . . ."

T. D. Kemp, Jr., a regular columnist for the *Charlotte Observer*, ran the Southern Attractions booking agency. Dad and I used to visit in his office about family dates, and we were always impressed with the way Mr. Kemp could keep two conversations going at the same time into the two telephones on his desk, a receiver at each ear!

Another person responsible for several of our show dates was Wally Fowler of Nashville, Tennessee. In addition to being head of a publishing company, he is considered the originator of all-night singings. Wally booked the family for such shows in Columbia, South Carolina, and Asheville, North Carolina, for example. A number of other groups would also be on these programs.

These singings would begin at eight o'clock in the evening and last until around four in the morning! We never wanted to go on first; furthermore, we believed in singing as little as possible. "Leave them wanting more," Dad told us. Our main concern in these all-night singings was that groups preceding us not perform some popular song that we had planned to include in our segment, such as Stuart Hamblen's "It Is No Secret."

Across the years I had forgotten how the family started recording for Columbia Records. When I asked Dad about this, he replied, "You've heard it said that a rabbit's foot is lucky." He went on to tell me that a rabbit's foot was really responsible for the Columbia contract. "I was going up on the elevator in the Wilder Building," he told me, "when a man asked, 'Do I not see a rabbit's foot sticking out of your bag?' 'Yep! you sure do,' I answered. 'It's a wild rabbit. We trap lots of them where we live.'"

The elevator conversation continued. "I haven't eaten a wild rabbit since I was with my grandmother down in Alabama," the gentleman continued. "What do you do with them?"

"Sell them," my father replied. "How much?" the man continued. "Fifty cents," Dad replied. My father gave him one.

Several days passed. Dad was at the station switchboard, talking with the receptionist when this same man came by. "That rabbit sure was good!" he said. When he left, my father asked about the man's position at the station and was told that he was the new station manager, A. D. Willard, who had recently arrived from WTOP in Washington, D. C.

"When I went back to Mr. Willard's office," my father continued, "he asked,

'What do you do besides trap rabbits?' I then told him about the family and he promised to listen to our next Sunday morning program. On Monday, I was back in his office, where he told me how much he liked our singing. 'Have you ever recorded?' he asked. 'Recorded what?' I asked. 'Have you ever made any records?' I told him we had not.

" 'You ought to be on records,' Mr. Willard said flatly. When I asked how, he said simply, 'I'll take care of that.' Jess Willard then reached for his phone and called 'Uncle Art' Satherly at Columbia Records in New York. When he finally reached him in California, I heard him say, 'Art, I want you to come to Charlotte. There's a family here that needs to be on records.' " Mr. Satherly promised to come the following week and asked that the family meet with him when he arrived.

On Wednesday of the next week, Art Satherly and his associate, Don Law, both showed up at WBT. As we auditioned for them, I saw Art give an "okay" sign to Mr. Law in the control room. Both men impressed us with their directions during the recording sessions. Not until I read an obituary notice about Mr. Satherly's death in 1986, however, did I learn about his intimate knowledge of the business.

Born in Bristol, England, in 1889, Satherly had come to America in 1912 "to see the cowboys and Indians" but ended up working as a secretary for Thomas Edison. Through Edison, who invented the incandescent lamp and the phonograph, Satherly got involved with the early development of the recording industry. He later became a country music talent scout and was the first to sign and record Gene Autry; he also recorded Roy Rogers, Tex Ritter, Roy Acuff, the original Carter Family, Little Jimmy Dickens, Red Foley, Leftie Frizzell, Bill Monroe and Marty Robbins.

If I had known at the time of Mr. Satherly's connections with Thomas Edison, I'm sure I would have "picked his brain" about the famous inventor and duly reported my findings in high school and college composition/research papers!

Today, the artist cards in the Columbia Records archives show that between 1946 and 1953, the family recorded a total of fifty-two songs on twenty-six different 78 rpm records (see discography). In addition to the singles released, we had EP's (extended play) and albums that included selections from the 78's and Betty's solos. Dad's rabbit foot paid off in more ways than one!

In looking over old royalty statements recently, I was interested to see that our best-selling records were the early ones. At our initial session in Charlotte on April 1, 1946, we cut eight sides. A royalty earnings summary from Columbia, dated 06–30–47, shows that "Cabin in the Valley of the Pines" and "I'll Reap My Harvest in Heaven" sold 59,934 records. "Sunday Morning in Dixie" and "He Put the Sunshine in My Soul" sold 33,062 copies. Our royalty check for those two records alone came to $1,673.94.

The 12–31–47 statement showed some decline. In this six-month period, "Cabin in the Valley of the Pines" and "I'll Reap My Harvest in Heaven" sold 2,037 copies. "Sunday Morning in Dixie" and "He Put the Sunshine in My Soul" sold 125 copies; "Wait for the Light to Shine" and "The Old Family Bible" sold 12,515 copies. Gross royalty earnings for this period came to only $264.20.

Perhaps these sales were the best because of the scarcity of records following World War II, when shellac was in short supply.

With the added income from record sales, Dad proceeded to purchase thirteen acres of land from "Goat" and Cora Taylor. The tract lay behind Oakdale Elementary School, at the end of a dirt road overlooking an artificial lake. Mother and Dad insisted on calling the road Possum Walk—the name of the old Pleasant Grove Road. In the early 1970s, Mother pushed unsuccessfully for a legal name change but, in the end, had to settle for Cora Avenue. We built a lovely three-bedroom house, with a full-sized basement and patio. I claimed the den, where I had a desk and a couch that also served as a bed. A fireplace in the basement made that part of the house a favorite spot for get-togethers.

We learned one important lesson in building our house on "Johnson Hill." Never bother a bulldozer! One Sunday afternoon we thought we could help move the project along by pushing over some stumps. Dad was the driver and, unfortunately, the bulldozer broke down. We had to shell out for the repairs. Having led our unauthorized use of the equipment, Dad announced the obvious to my brothers and me: "Let's not do *that* again!"

We turned to our neighbor, Parris Hipp, for a loan to complete the house. The year before, we had moved into a pretty bungalow owned by radio station WAYS. The "transmitter house" had running water and central heating, which made our lives there seem luxurious. After Will Elliott completed our house on "Johnson Hill" in 1946, we moved into our first real home.

I was not aware of any anxiety on Dad's part about the cost of the new house. Recently, however, I ran across a notation he had made on one of our radio scripts which indicated some uneasiness. The program aired on October 19, 1947, and was a fifteen-minute Sunday morning sustaining show on CBS. (The term "sustaining show" means that there was no sponsor for it, and that the money the station paid us was minimal.) At the top of each radio script sheet were eight blanks, one of them reading "agency." In that blank, Dad had written, "We are hoping." This was a not-so-subtle hint for station management to work harder in finding us a sponsor.

Songs about hope were a primary theme of that program and many others. While the earlier part of Dad's life may have lacked any formal religious connections, the songs we sang contained the biblical message of hope. This undoubtedly affected my father's attitude.

When the family broke up in 1951, the house was almost paid for. The final payment was made in 1954, thanks again to the common bank account and faithful work by Bob, Jim, Betty, and my parents. During this particular period, I was involved with my college work and a student pastorate.

One surprising spinoff from our work with Columbia Records was the song-writing efforts of my parents. Dad was not the best businessman in the world, so one cannot always be certain of the sequence of some of his song contracts. Based on the records I have, it seems that my father wrote ten songs, six of which were recorded by Columbia:

"Somebody's Waiting for Me" — Columbia 20426
Recording date: December 28, 1947
Publisher: Wallace Fowler Pub., May 24, 1949; later assigned to Cross and Crown Music Co.

"Grandma's Spinning Wheel" — Columbia 20589
Recording date: May 4, 1949
Publisher: Wallace Fowler Pub., May 13, 1949

"The Old Country Church at the Foot of the Hill" — Columbia 20653–s
Recording date: May 4, 1949
Publisher: Wallace Fowler Pub., May 13, 1949

"You Left Me Cryin' in the Rain"
Publisher: Wallace Fowler Pub., May 13, 1949

"I Like the Old-Time Way" — Columbia 20838
Recording date: May 7, 1951
Publisher: Cross and Crown Music, April 13, 1950

"Dear Mother"
Publisher: Initially Wallace Fowler Pub., May 24, 1949; canceled by mutual agreement May 4, 1950
Assigned to Cross and Crown April 20, 1950, under the title "My Mother"

"He Will Pay All the Cost"
Publisher: Initially Wallace Fowler Pub., May 24, 1949; canceled by mutual agreement
May 4, 1950
Assigned to Cross and Crown April 20, 1950

"Reunion in the Sky" — Columbia 20759
Recording date: June 23, 1950
Publisher: Peer International Corp.

"Round the Old Log Cabin"
Publisher: Composed by Larry Walker but published under Dad's name; assigned undated
to Cross and Crown Music

"The Death of Ellenton" — Columbia 20895
Publisher: Unknown
Writers: According to the Columbia record label, Dad cowrote this song with Dixie
Smith.

Mother is credited with two songs:

"Little Cabin on the Hill"
Publisher: Initially Wallace Fowler Pub., May 13, 1949; canceled May 4, 1950
Assigned to Cross and Crown, April 20, 1950

"I've Got a Feeling" — Columbia 20536
Recording date: December 28, 1947
Publisher: Initially Wallace Fowler Pub., May 24, 1949; canceled May 4, 1950
Assigned to Cross and Crown, April, 1950

Some of my parents' song-writing ability rubbed off on my brothers, Bob and
Jim. Today Bob has hanging on the wall in his home Columbia 20759. On one
side is Dad's composition "Reunion in the Sky" and on the other is "I Have Got
Old-Time Religion," written by Bob and Jim.

That a husband-and-wife team who had never completed the elementary grades
could use their creative talents to compose music for a nationally known family of
singers amazed me! Of course, my parents never claimed excellence as lyricists
or as musicians, yet their down-home compositions blended in with the family's
singing. I am reminded that neither Betty nor I, with our educational advantages,
ever came up with a single composition for the family!

During the thirteen years of our entertainment career, we went through three
different name changes. We started out in 1938 simply as the Johnson Family.

A new station manager who came to WBT from the North in the early 1940s thought that "Ma" Johnson's Family had a more commercial tone and would draw, no doubt, upon the popularity of another radio celebrity named "Ma" Perkins. The new name lasted only a year or so and was carried on several promotional pieces, but none of us liked it. By the mid-1940s, the Johnson Family Singers had evolved, and the name remained with us for the rest of our career.

The most lucrative contract of our singing career was a regional CBS program sponsored by the Quaker Oats Company. The program had no name as such. We simply referred to it as our "Quaker Corn Meal Program." Larry Walker was pianist for these shows, assisted by Arthur Smith on the guitar. Ken Tredwell was the producer. Dad is credited with composing the theme song, but it was actually written by Larry Walker. The program opened with a rhythmic guitar introduction, followed by the piano and the family singing our signature song:

> When the family gets together 'round the old log cabin,
>> The sound of voices singing fills the air;
> When they start to harmonizing 'round the old log cabin,
>> You'll never find a worry or a care.

We were even able to locate an authentic log cabin, around which we made innumerable publicity pictures for the program. Whenever we had personal appearances, Bob and Jim worked a Quaker Oats display. On stage, they presented a bag of Quaker Corn Meal to the youngest and oldest persons present and to the person coming the greatest distance to our program.

We had other family network shows that originated from WBT but, for the most part, they were broadcast without sponsorship. These paid minimum wage, whereas the Quaker shows brought us around three hundred dollars a week, a far cry from the ten-dollar weekly salary in the early 1940s! The Quaker series started in January 1950, and concluded in May 1951, when the contract was suddenly canceled because of Quaker's decision to shift its advertising budget from radio to newspapers.

Throughout our career at WBT our agreements with management had been verbal until the Quaker Oats shows, when we signed a contract with Richard Maxwell of Geruth Enterprises, New York, to be our manager. This management arrangement didn't go well with WBT officials, but it did result in additional income for the family. In retrospect, I suspect both the family and station officials would have been happier if we had simply continued with our verbal agreements.

We always felt good about our friendships at WBT. Charles Crutchfield, whom we first knew as the *Briarhopper* announcer, then as program director and, finally, as station manager, always had a kind word for us. Hovie Lister, pianist for the Rangers Quartet, came to WBT in the middle of 1946 and remained through 1947, before leaving to establish the Statesmen Quartet in 1948. While his work did not relate directly to the family, Jack Nell, who for years was the station news director, was a good friend, as was announcer Clyde McClain. Studio engineers—"big" Buster Richardson, "calm" Tommy Callahan, and "dry" Ralph Painter—all had a hand in shaping our career.

Three out-of-town engagements were especially memorable. One was a guest appearance on the Grand Ole Opry in Nashville, where at the old Ryman Auditorium we met the hillbilly greats of the day. We had made several appearances in the Carolinas with Bill Monroe and his Bluegrass Boys. It was good to be with them in Nashville as well as to meet Roy Acuff, Ernest Tubb, and Minnie Pearl. On one occasion, Bob and Jim were driven from their hotel to a recording studio by Hank Williams in his big Cadillac.

During the 1948 presidential campaign, when Strom Thurmond ran as a third-party candidate, we entertained for the senator at a political rally in Cherryville, where Blaine Beam put on a huge watermelon slicing. I was not aware that in the crowd that night were some local schoolteachers, including a recent arrival from Union, South Carolina, whom I would meet and marry three years later!

After graduating from Harding High School in 1947, Betty went to Queens College in Charlotte and I to Davidson, a liberal arts college twenty miles north. This kept both of us close to the family radio shows. While at Queens, a romance blossomed between Betty and a Davidson football coach, Dick Redding, and they were married in 1949. Clarence Etter, staff organist at WBT, played for the wedding at Pleasant Grove Methodist Church, which secured a new electronic organ for the occasion. Bob and Jim and I sang.

Betty joined First Presbyterian Church in Charlotte; I became a member of Dilworth Methodist Church. Nevertheless, Pleasant Grove came to be the family church, with my parents and brothers being charter members when the new sanctuary was constructed in 1949. The influence of my Sunday School teacher there, Parks Dunn, was especially important during my growing years, as was the help of various pastors: Dr. Howard P. Powell, J. Leonard Rayle, John W. Carter, Jack H. Cooke, and M. Arthur Lewis.

The day of June 24, 1951, stands out especially in my memory. Even though

I was attending summer school at Duke University at the time, I traveled back to Charlotte to join the family for an engagement at the annual "Singing on the Mountain" at Grandfather Mountain. People were there by the thousands. Their enthusiasm for our music was obvious from their applause. It was a festive and happy occasion, one that was to be our last family engagement for several years, a time during which Betty moved to New York, Bob and Jim worked as pages at NBC in that city, and I was ordained as a Methodist pastor.

Mother and Dad were left alone on "Johnson Hill" that summer, where they tried to sort out their singing strategies for the days ahead. Looking back over our music career, Dad once said, "We had a rough, hard row to hoe, but we made it. Good things don't come on a silver platter. You gotta work for them. Then you appreciate the good things in life. When you get to the place you don't have to worry about making a living, then you appreciate the tough times."

There is an inevitable breakup in every family circle, a time when the apron strings untie and children move out in search of lives for themselves, finding their own careers and fulfilling their own destinies. Sooner or later, most children get married and go their separate ways. Mothers and fathers approach this day with understandable apprehension, and, when it happens, grief is inevitable for all who are involved. Children have not only to adjust to the pain of separation but to the challenge of their own careers. Parents and children alike must travel roads they have not traveled before.

Since our childhoods had been so intimately involved with the work of our parents, the transition to separate lives was even more difficult than it is for many. Our parents saw the family reduced from six back to the two who had started singing as a couple before the family group was formed at a Greensboro apartment in 1938. This was not an easy transition for them.

CHANGES IN THE FAMILY CIRCLE

Parents tend to look to the past, while children become immersed in the present. No one in our family had seemed to anticipate the day when the children would leave and begin their own families. "Surely 'Ma' and 'Pa' Johnson must have known that the day would come when their nest would be emptied," the outsider might say. If my parents entertained such thoughts, they never discussed them with us. Instead, they put as much time and energy into our family music career during our young adult years as they had done when we were children.

Even when Betty married Dick Redding in August of 1949, my parents were reluctant to concede any basic change in the family's music career. Although Betty moved with her husband into an apartment just off the Davidson campus, she continued singing with us on radio and in out-of-town appearances.

The second traumatic break in the family circle came two years later, in the summer of 1951, when I showed my father my local preacher's license. Inasmuch as his childhood friend, Dr. Edgar H. Nease—then the district superintendent of the Charlotte district of the Methodist Church—had signed it, I thought it would make him glad. Instead, he mumbled, "I hope that'll do you some good!" Unable to acknowledge their feelings of anger over my going my own way, he and other family members initially resented my joining the Methodist ministry. Dad once asked, "Son, why are you leaving the family?" I replied, "Dad, in a real sense I'm not leaving the family. . . . I'm building onto the family!" He didn't get it.

The family was disappointed about my leaving partly because I had been doing strategic work, serving as director, producer, and even secretary-treasurer. This loss of a significant relationship caused them to grieve and, as therapists know, their grief contained an element of anger. I understood their feelings but was helpless to do anything about it.

We all have our own identities and must fulfill our own destinies. We are shaped by our genes and environment, but finding our gifts and using them at the point of interest and/or need is a challenge facing the individual. Mother and Dad, bless their memory, failed to anticipate their children's need to enter the world of adult living, which included our getting married. In some ways, bringing other persons into the family circle seemed to them like an intrusion, especially when they discovered that the newcomers didn't sing or share our musical interests! As it turned out, these additions to the family appreciated our music and encouraged us to pursue the family work.

I have not said much thus far about the religious side of the family's life, even though we are remembered mostly for our gospel singing. Frankly, we were so busy singing the faith that as a whole we spent little time nurturing it! An exception to this situation occurred when the family moved to Charlotte and most of us became part of Pleasant Grove Methodist Church.

The formal side of my religious instruction did not begin until 1943, when I was fifteen. During my midteens, I started attending Sunday School and worship regularly at the old Pleasant Grove Church nearby. Occasionally we would have schedule conflicts between a family engagement and church activity—such as a CBS program on Sunday mornings at 9:45—but generally I was able to do both. Sometimes we would have a show in Asheville or Columbia or some other town and would not return home until the early hours on Sunday, yet I would still make it to church. Because of the church's importance to me, I was baptized and joined in August 1947. A year later, my parents and brothers also became an official part of the Pleasant Grove Church family. (Earlier, when Betty was fifteen, she had broken the Methodist ranks to join the Presbyterian Church, where she has remained. For years she has been an elder in the Fifth Avenue Presbyterian Church in New York City.)

During the years when I was between the ages of fifteen and twenty-three, my religious interests were focused especially on choral music. At the same time, I was developing a special interest in writing and English literature. At Davidson College, I majored in English and qualified for a high school teacher's certificate. But a religious struggle during my junior year resulted in my entering the Methodist ministry.

During the winter of 1950–1951, thoughts of pastoral ministry began to pull at me. Alongside this struggle was my being in love with and wanting to marry an eighth-grade teacher at Paw Creek High School. When I said "yes" to both concerns in April of 1951, my separation from the family became inevitable. At the same time, I experienced a peace of mind and sense of direction that have remained constant across more than forty-three years of marriage and ministry.

On Thanksgiving Day, 1951, while in my senior year at Davidson College, Evelyn Guyton and I were married at her home church in Union, South Carolina. Dad was my best man. Partly because of my plans for marriage, I was appointed a student pastor of the McKendree Charge seven weeks before Thanksgiving. I studied, did practice teaching at North Mecklenburg High School, and preached at McKendree Chapel, Williamson's Chapel, and Rocky Mount. Meanwhile, the rest of my family continued singing in churches and at veterans' hospitals across the Southeast. Betty was following two tracks, being in New York for solo recordings and appearances and in between joining Mother, Dad and the twins for some of their performances. Because of my studies and pastoral duties, I was with them only on rare occasions.

The family started recording for RCA-Victor on September 21, 1954. Betty had visited the offices of Trinity Music in Manhattan. Trinity was affiliated with BMI and operated by Joe Csida (a former *Billboard* editor) and Charles Grean (an RCA-Victor executive). Grean took an immediate interest in Betty and the family. Between 1954 and 1959, the family recorded a total of forty different selections, released as singles or as albums, for RCA-Victor (see discography for dates of the recording sessions and the selections).

The RCA-Victor series reveals important changes in the Johnson sound. The first three recording sessions show some dilution of the family's familiar sound. I was unable to join them for these sessions because of my classes in the Duke Divinity School and my duties in two small churches, New Mt. Vernon and Shady Grove. Least representative of the family sound are the songs recorded by Dad, Betty, and two extra singers, Betty Dillard and William G. Wright, Jr., in session 5 on November 11, 1956.

The entire family assembled in Nashville on Monday, June 29, 1959, for our fifth and final recording session for RCA-Victor. We recorded sixteen hymns, several of which were augmented by two or three other pick-up singers. Charles Grean, who had promoted Betty's records on several labels, was the mastermind behind these recordings; he was anxious to make us sound like a church choir in several of the selections. Chet Atkins, local RCA-Victor artist and repertoire representative, also assisted in the production. The LPM-2126 album, which featured these selections, also contains a copy of the text of each of the hymns and some candid photos of the family made during the session. (These sixteen numbers were recorded between 2:30 and 11:30 P.M.; we were exhausted afterwards.)

One other matter of interest on the LPM-2126 album is the cover picture of the family. The stained-glass picture backdrop was made in the balcony of a Lutheran Church in Nashville, near the United Methodist Publishing House building. The same picture was used in an RCA Camden 816 release, "Old-Time Religion," in 1964. The Camden album featured the Johnson Family Singers, the Carter Family, and the Speer Family and included four Johnson selections (titles are noted in the discography).

Appropriately, the last recorded song by the family for RCA-Victor in Nashville contained the words "God be with you 'til we meet again." The family breakup, which had started ten years before, was about to be completed. Betty continued her solo work in New York; Bob pursued a brief career as a professional in the Boy Scouts; Jim was doing sales work; I was involved in pastoral ministry. Nevertheless, the Johnson Family Singers came together for two other television events in July 1965.

The first was a TV recording session called "The Best of Country & Western Music" with Eddy Arnold in Chicago. Our daughter, Martha Lynn Ballard, recently found a copy of the script for the program in a scrapbook she had kept as a child. The first page contains the following information:

THEME: DOLPH'S BREAKDOWN
SQUARE DANCING, PEOPLE FILING IN, SHOUTING AND HAVING A GOOD TIME.

ANNCR: Ladies and gentlemen, welcome to THE BEST OF COUNTRY & WESTERN MUSIC, starring
    The Tennessee Plowboy, Eddy Arnold,
    Miss Minnie Pearl,
    Betty Johnson and the Johnson Family,
    The Grammy Award Winner, Miss Dottie West,
    The Collins Kids,
    Bob Atcher,
    Arkie and the Champion Dixon Dancers,
    and the Sage Riders!

On the final page were the autographs obtained by twelve-year-old Martha Lynn: Eddy Arnold, John Frigo, Dottie West, Red Blanchard, Larry Collins, Bob Atcher, and Minnie Pearl. Our daughter insisted on keeping the original script but provided me with a copy.

The second event was a live TV program with Mike Douglas who, at that time, originated his program in Cleveland, Ohio. During the show, Mother called on our three children to sing "On Moonlight Bay" with her! She loved teaching them to sing and showing them off. In one of the family numbers, we were flattered to be joined by another guest on the program, Tony Bennett.

Betty, with typical thoughtfulness and generosity, brought together the family for Bob and Jim's thirty-second birthday celebration at a Cleveland hotel the next day, July 13, 1965. This turned out to be the final family gathering in which every member was present.

After Betty and I graduated from Harding High School in 1947, Bob and Jim transferred back to Paw Creek High for their final three years, graduating in 1951. At Paw Creek they became cheerleaders and were instrumental in acquainting me with an eighth-grade teacher, Evelyn Guyton, teacher-advisor to the cheerleaders who had recently arrived there from the Cherryville school system.

My identical-twin brothers took delight in being misidentified and playing pranks on unsuspecting people. One such incident occurred when Bob was scheduled for surgery. During a period of testing beforehand, Jim came by late in the afternoon, changed into Bob's hospital gown, and climbed into bed, pretending to be his brother. While the older twin was out on the town for dinner, Jim ate Bob's hospital meal and even took his medication! Not anticipating the effects of this playful stunt, Bob returned to his room later in the evening to find Jim sound asleep! They made a quick shift before the nurse came in for the next temperature reading.

One sensitive area for both Jim and Bob as young adults was their ineligibility for the draft. While their peers were being drafted into the army for the Korean conflict, they were both turned down after three days of extensive testing at Fort Bragg showed "limited eye perception." Given 4-F status, they went to New York, where Betty was, and were employed as pages at NBC.

After a year or so in the Big Apple, the twins returned to Charlotte to join Mother and Dad for a singing tour with Veterans Hospital Programs, a Protestant-sponsored group. An all-girl trio was also part of the tour. Bob was instantly attracted to one of them—Mary L. Sloan—and after a brief courtship, they were married in 1956. This left Jim as the lone single at home.

After working a short time with Duke Power Company, saving all he made for his college education, Bob enrolled at the University of North Carolina at Chapel Hill for some special courses in radio and television. This was followed by a job in television at WBTV in Charlotte. Bob and Mary doubled the number of grandchildren for Mother and Dad with the birth of three lovely children: Robert Deverin, Betty Jean, and Ginger Lee.

"On my nights off," Bob recalled, "I was active as cubmaster for Pack 51 of the Boy Scouts of America. In this work I could see boys grow up and through motivation and training become leaders—an experience I had missed while growing up." This scouting interest resulted in Bob's becoming a full-time district scout executive. After several years as a professional scouter, which Bob considers the most satisfying work of his adult life, he became a moving consultant. In more recent years, he has received his real estate license and has worked in real estate and management.

Perhaps more than any other family member, Bob has always been interested in domestic life—gardening, cooking, and piddling about the house. He and Jim were regular visitors to Mother and Dad's, where he would automatically jump into mowing or plowing or gardening or work in the kitchen—whatever was needed. He was divorced in 1978 but has tried to maintain cordial relations with his family.

In the early fifties Jim and Bob were students at Davidson, Queens, and Roanoke College, before Jim transferred to the University of Miami in 1957. While getting his degree at Miami, Jim met an attractive Swedish girl named Sonja Nelson, whom he married in 1961. To this union were born four children: Bryan, Leandra, Lisa, and Lara. Unfortunately, his marriage also ended in separation and divorce in 1977. Meanwhile, his ties of fatherly affection have continued unabated.

Jim was the second Johnson to graduate from college, receiving an A. B. degree in radio-television production from the University of Miami in 1960. Unfortunately, his activity in sales in the years that followed was unrelated to radio or television. In his varied vocational pursuits, Jim leads all the family members in number and types of employment! Prominent among his early experiences was tourism development. He also had broad experience in chamber of commerce work, mass advertising, and fund-raising, including a stint with President Carter's inaugural committee in 1976–1977. For several years now, Jim has boasted of being president of the Can Do Company, which consists primarily of a private courier service.

Untying the apron strings was especially hard for Betty. (I mentioned earlier how she had combined marriage and music before the breakup of the Johnson Family Singers in the early fifties.) In the fall of 1951, Betty went with Mother and Dad and the twins to Wheeling, West Virginia, for an engagement with the Veterans' Hospital Programs. Singing for crippled and disabled veterans was quite emotional and depressing for her, so, one October night, she slipped into a telephone booth in the hotel lobby and called Percy Faith, whom she had met at the final family

Columbia Records session the previous June. He had told her, "If you ever want to try it on your own, let me know." Percy was an A&R executive at Columbia Records and a talented arranger for many singers, including Rosemary Clooney, Johnny Mathis, and Doris Day. He was also the able composer of such songs as "My Heart Cries for You" and many others.

Shortly after returning home from a trip to Charleston, Betty left the family and moved into the Girls' Performing Arts Club on the Upper West Side in New York. "When I got there," she confessed to Terry Gross in an interview on National Public Radio's popular *Fresh Air*, "I did nothing but cry. I was so lonely . . . the promise of New York failed to replace the comfort of working with family . . . we did everything together. We worked the farm together. We worked in the studio together. We worked personal appearances together. So being alone for the first time was God-awful."

While Betty's husband, Dick, occupied himself with Davidson football, and the Johnson Family Singers were adjusting to quartet size, Betty auditioned for and won a spot on *Arthur Godfrey's Talent Scouts*. As a winner there, she was entitled to a week's appearance on Godfrey's CBS morning show; in addition, she became a featured singer on the Saturday morning *Galen Drake Show*.

By and large, during the fifties Betty tried to fill the void left by our family's breakup while establishing her own identity as a singer. Failing to find fulfillment in her marriage, she tried to find it in her music career. Her rise to fame and fortune had hardly begun when, on a New Year's visit with her husband in Connecticut, she became pregnant. "I really thought my career had ended," she said later.

Betty moved into the Martha Washington Hotel and walked two miles uptown to her engagement as a production singer at the Copacabana Night Club. She never told her fellow performers that she was pregnant. In March she gave notice to the management and returned to her apartment in Davidson. Even before Harold Richard Redding, Jr., was born on September 15, 1952, though, her marriage was showing signs of strain.

After the birth of Dick, Jr., Betty's husband resigned from his position at Davidson College to become backfield coach at Virginia Polytechnic Institute in Blacksburg, Virginia. Because of her radio commitments and other engagements in the New York area, Betty traveled there frequently from Blacksburg. As a result, Mother often pitched in as babysitter and nurse to the growing grandson. My sister resumed her career over CBS with *On a Sunday Afternoon* and *There's Music in the Air*. In addition to these programs, she started producing the "Borden Girl" commercials for Young & Rubican Advertising Agency.

The early fifties were traumatic years for Betty, who was torn between family and career. Unhappily, her marriage ended in divorce, and her sense of parental responsibility vied with her commitment to her career. Even though she gave her husband custody of their son—the only way he would agree to a divorce—Betty visited and kept in touch with the child on a consistent basis. She proved to be an excellent absentee mother, despite her accelerated entertainment career. Betty and her present husband, Arthur, continue to maintain a close relationship with her son.

Betty met Charles Grean and Joe Csida, former editor of *Billboard*, at Trinity Music in New York in June 1954. Within weeks, Grean had become Betty's manager and had begun to provide real impetus for her work, especially her recordings. Having won out over fourteen other contestants in auditions for *Don McNeil's Breakfast Club* some months later, she moved to Chicago and became a regular on that radio program for two years. She also continued as a frequent guest on *Eddy Arnold Time*, a TV series.

Betty's first solo recordings, which she did in 1951 and 1952 after the family's sessions were completed, were for Columbia. On CL 1177, *Faith of Our Fathers,* we have a combination of family numbers and solos by Betty. A similar Columbia 45 EP, B 11772 vol. 2, combines Betty's solos with two family favorites: "Farther Along" (Col. 20867) and "Whispering Hope" (Col. 21180-s).

After her Columbia and RCA-Victor recordings with the family, Betty turned to other labels. Her first Atlantic album was entitled simply *Betty Johnson*. It was recorded and released in the fall of 1956. Also in October of that year, she made a week-long guest appearance on the NBC-TV soap opera *Modern Romance*, where she launched her hit record, "I Dreamed." On December 16, 1957, she appeared with Jack Paar on the Ed Sullivan Show. This started a friendship that would culminate in her becoming a regular on Jack Paar's *The Tonight Show*.

In 1957 while Betty's career zoomed forward, she became less involved with the family. Within the first two months of the year, she had appeared on national television with such notables as Will Rogers, Jr., George Gobel, Jonathan Winters, Vaughan Monroe, and Ed Sullivan. In March, she concluded her two-year contract with *Don McNeil's Breakfast Club* and moved back to New York, where she appeared with Louis Armstrong, including one show at the Roxy Theater, for an extended engagement. Her "Little White Lies" and "I Dreamed" were climbing high on the record charts, and in July Jack Paar hired her as a regular for his show. That summer *Cash Box* magazine voted her "The Nation's Most Promising Girl Singer."

On October 4, 1957, Betty married her manager, Charles Grean, at her Greenwich Village apartment. After their European honeymoon, she returned to the Paar show. In addition to her numerous TV appearances and radio shows, she found time for dates at political conventions, hotels, and clubs. The day after an appearance before the National Press Club in Washington, D. C., Betty came to the Rotary Club in Asheboro, North Carolina; at this time, she was also doing a nightly stint at the Plantation Supper Club in Greensboro.

I began this story of my family by recalling those two memorable Sullivan appearances in March of 1958. The Sunday edition of the *New York Times* for March 2, 1958, carried an article by John P. Shanley entitled "Singer from Dixie" and subtitled "Betty Johnson of Possum Walk Road Finds Success on Television." The story included a picture of "Betty Johnson, whose songs are gaining wide popularity." Ben Gross's *Times* column on March 3 read, "Betty Johnson and her singing family contributed some heart-warming moments during Ed Sullivan's segment devoted to Southern music . . . Betty's a great ad for her family and vice versa."

In August of 1958, Betty broadened her singing career to include acting, playing the part of Teddy in *Wish You Were Here* at the Theater-Under-the-Stars in Atlanta. The August 18, 1958, issue of *Time* magazine carried a picture of Jack Paar on the cover and a writeup about Betty on page fifty-three. A series of state fairs and parades, including the Carolinas Carrousel in Charlotte, completed her year. By the third decade of her life she was established nationally as a pop singer and was in constant demand at state fairs and clubs across the nation. She also became the first American to appear on Danish television.

Whereas in the fifties Betty was establishing her identity as a pop singer, the next decade was for her a period of maturation and spiritual growth. Her acting skills were on view in an increasing number of appearances in summer stock, including the role of Nellie Forbush in *South Pacific*, performed in New York State (Syracuse and Rochester) in July 1960.

During all of her activity, Betty never forgot her family members. She and Mother were often together for appearances and on trips, and she always found time to write letters and send us gifts. She never missed birthdays! In addition, she would arrange to attend important family events, such as Jim's graduation from the University of Miami at Coral Gables in June 1960, and my receiving a doctorate at Drew University in October 1981. She was also financial sponsor for several important church trips, including my attendance at the general conferences of 1956, 1960, 1964, and 1968. Her most ambitious financial backing came when I was selected as a member of the Mission to British Methodism team in the spring of 1962.

As Betty's career continued to be active, I began to notice in her letters signs of marital stress. Whereas her first marriage floundered because of the partners' incompatibility, the marriage to Charles suffered from neglect. "We were so busy with our careers," my sister once told me, "that we really never got to know each other!" Even after her decision to sever business relations with Charles, matters didn't improve. Annual trips to Europe or the Orient failed to stave off the disintegration. While Charles made important contributions to Betty's music career, the two were unable to make a success of their marriage, and it ended during the final days of 1961.

In 1962, Betty and Mother recorded an album of hymns. Their label was Super Recordings, Glen Ellyn, Illinois. For the cover, my sister used a picture of her and mother which had first appeared in the *Greensboro Daily News* in 1956. Each sold the record in various gatherings and placed the money in a special savings account in Mother's name.

Betty set attendance records at Charlotte's Summer Theater, where she played to sell-out audiences. The series began with her role as Nellie Forbush in *South Pacific* in 1963, followed by that of Maria Rainier in *The Sound of Music* in 1964. In 1965, it was *The King and I*, and in 1966 Mother came back early from a European trip with us to see Betty's concluding performance in *Finian's Rainbow*.

In April 1963, Governor Terry Sanford honored prominent North Carolinians in the field of entertainment by presenting them each with a sterling silver bowl. Although she was playing an engagement at the Sands Hotel in Las Vegas at the time and could not attend the ceremony, Betty was pleased to be included in this recognition alongside such notables as Edward R. Murrow, Sidney Blackmer, David Brinkley, and Ava Gardner.

On December 26, 1961, Betty had opened a three-week return engagement at the Coconut Grove in Los Angeles, where at a New Year's Eve party she was introduced to a successful Wall Street investment banker, Arthur Gray, Jr., a man of unusual maturity and judgment. After a courtship of a little more than two years, they were married at the Fifth Avenue Presbyterian Church in New York City on May 4, 1964. Two lovely daughters, Lydia and Elisabeth, were to be born in succeeding years. As her family responsibilities increased, Betty began to shift her music career to a position of second place.

In addition to Betty's growth and development in marriage, I began to see other signs of progress. Dr. Maria Negy, a New York psychologist and a member of Madison Avenue Presbyterian Church, gave her important help, as did Dr. Bryant M. Kirkland, senior minister at the Fifth Avenue Presbyterian Church, who arrived in New York at about the same time that Betty started attending that church. He was able to nurture Betty and Arthur in their courtship, and he officiated at their marriage in the chapel at Fifth Avenue. Betty had transferred from First Presbyterian, New York City, and Arthur joined her later by profession of faith.

Arthur Gray, Jr., began to assume important leadership roles in the church at Fifth Avenue, as deacon, elder, trustee, and as manager of the church's endowment portfolio, which increased dramatically in value during his tenure as a trustee. His fellow members praised him for his leadership in obtaining long-range improvement funds for the church. Betty also performed important services for the church, heading their altar flower committee and later being elected an elder, a member of the session, and a member of the pulpit search committee.

Whereas her career and marriage had been Betty's primary concerns during the sixties, in the next decade her career took a secondary position to the responsibilities of motherhood. To nurture their daughters, Lydia and Elisabeth, who had been born in 1966 and 1968, Betty and Arthur moved to Maple Hill Farm in Pound Ridge, New York. While this location required that Arthur commute for two hours in the morning and at night, it gave the children an unhurried, pleasant atmosphere in which to grow up. At Pound Ridge, Betty's homemaking skills were to be seen in the magnificent gardens and in her interests in needlepoint, gardening, canning and flower arranging. Winning blue ribbons at fairs and flower shows got to be commonplace. She became a master flower show judge in the Federated Garden Clubs of America. While her own family was her dominant interest, she kept in touch with the rest of us.

When our eldest son, Kenneth, Jr., found himself restive during his final year of high school, Betty sponsored him in a summer enrichment program at Exeter Academy. We visited him there in the summer of 1971, and Betty told me, "Brother, I don't see how with five children you've managed to live with only one car." She then handed me the keys to her Volvo and said, "It's yours!" Such generosity, a trait inherited from our mother and maternal grandmother, has been characteristic of her life.

Toward the end of the sixties, Betty and Arthur had also acquired a 160-acre farm near Lyme Center, New Hampshire, and named it Two Sisters' Farm. After a few years there, they purchased Bliss Tavern in Haverhill, which had been built in 1788 by Captain Joseph Bliss, the first postmaster appointed by President George

Washington for the state of New Hampshire. Bliss Tavern, located on the green in Haverhill, provided lodging for such notables as Daniel Webster, and was an underground railroad station for slaves who were escaping from the South and were en route to Canada and freedom in the years before emancipation. Evidence of this is seen in a tunnel leading from the tavern to the nearby Connecticut River. Bliss Tavern has been Betty and Arthur's primary residence since they moved there in the fall of 1976, though they spend much time in New York and winter in St. Croix, Virgin Islands.

To the joy of both families, Betty's son, Dick, and our daughter, Martha Lynn, attended Duke University, where each graduated in 1975. Martha Lynn remained at Duke and received her Master of Divinity degree in 1978. Betty's son, Dick, began working for Xerox, where he has been in management for several years. Because my sister and I are so close in age—only thirteen months apart—we have often shared each other's woes, especially during our children's adolescent years. Letters exchanged between Betty and me during this period are filled with empathy, especially for me, as we struggled at the task of parenting. Betty, my brothers, and I had grown up with structure provided by a studio clock; in contrast, our children came along during the sixties and seventies, with that period's culture of drugs and youth rebellion. Being parents was tough for most people then, including my wife and me.

In the early seventies, Betty enrolled as a special student at Dartmouth College, an hour's drive from her home in Haverhill. She completed her undergraduate work but, because of age, could not receive her degree there. Dartmouth, however, arranged for a courtesy graduation through the University of New Hampshire.

In the early 1990s, Betty renewed her singing career in a successful comeback with appearances in New York's Algonquin Hotel, which led to other engagements. She also involved Lydia and Elisabeth, now grown, in several compact disc releases—*Take Five Sessions Vol. I, A Family Affair, My Heart Sings, In the Garden*, and *Soft Lights & Sweet Music*. Thus, the Johnson Family Singers now stretch across three generations, covering a span of more than sixty years.

On Thanksgiving Day in 1978, Evelyn and I had the pleasure of entertaining Betty and Arthur and Dad at our Lake Junaluska retirement home, which Betty and Arthur had helped us to build in 1969–1970. The only sadness about the occasion was the fact that Mother couldn't be with us. Dad had had to hospitalize her in North Augusta for some short-term emotional problems. We all drove down to see her the next day. Little did we know that within a few months, she would slip away from us for good.

A MEMORABLE
GOOD FRIDAY

A fter Betty had married and then later moved to New York to continue her career, the twins joined Mother and Dad in appearances at veterans' hospitals. In between these events and recording sessions, my mother kept the home fires burning for a dwindling number of people on what we called Johnson Hill in the Oakdale section of Charlotte. While she was learning to cook for fewer people, Dad was pursuing a different line of work—radio announcing!

Radio stations in the North Carolina cities of Charlotte, Belmont, and Canton, as well as in Lake City, South Carolina, had used my father's deep voice before he found his place at Station WDIX in Orangeburg in 1958. He played records, gave the news, weather, and reports, and ad-libbed his commercials. Sponsors lined up to be on his weekday morning programs, which were initially from seven o'clock until noon and later from nine till noon. During these shows, he played mainly country and western records (Jim Reeves was one of his favorite artists). On Sunday mornings from seven to nine, he played only religious music.

Dad always had time to play (and promote!) the family records. For example, he concluded his program for years with "May God Be With You," which was our RCA-Victor 47–6756 recording. Occasionally Mother, or one of the children visiting in Orangeburg, would go on his program to talk about the family.

Always the showman, Dad gave a commercial for himself at the conclusion of our workshop during the Charlotte Country Music Program at Spirit Square in October 1985: "If you're traveling down through South Carolina," he told the group, "I'm located in Orangeburg doing a radio show on WDIX. I've been there twenty-eight years. I retired there three weeks ago but I've decided to go back. I don't like retirement. So, I'll be back on the radio over WDIX, 1150 on your radio dial! You can pick me up across the creek, but when you leave you can't hear me. It's a weak station!" (Standing near Dad during his impromptu commercial was Betty, who added, "It may be a weak station but my father is a strong personality!")

For almost ten years, my parents kept the Charlotte house while establishing a second home in a trailer parked behind the WDIX transmitter. Initially Dad looked at the trailer as his independence. "If they want me to leave tomorrow," he said, "I can hitch up the trailer and move!" He would visit Charlotte occasionally; Mother would spend weeks with him at the trailer. When it became evident that his Orangeburg job was secure, they decided to sell the Charlotte house so they could build a brick one convenient to the transmitter. Real estate was selling slowly in Charlotte at the time, so my parents had to spend a great deal of time living in two states! All of the children were concerned about the separation. Finally, the house was sold; a new one was built, and they settled down in Orangeburg.

Before the move to South Carolina, our children had looked forward to visiting "Nannie" at the farm, where she won their hearts with her biscuits and where there was always a large tin of cookies on hand. Mother frequently visited Betty and was also the baby-sitter for various grandchildren, starting with Betty's son, Dickie, and continuing with my children and Bob and Jim's children. (I never knew this was such an exhausting role for grandparents until I became one!) My mother didn't mind helping with grandchildren, but she was reluctant to baby-sit during social activities. If there was to be a party, she wanted to be included!

Mother and Dad frequently got together for family reunions, fairs, commercials, and company dinners. They would dress up as "Ma" and "Pa," she in her denim dress and bonnet and he in his overalls and straw hat. In local parades they always drove in their attire, with a homemade sign on the side of the old pickup reading "Ma" and "Pa" Johnson. They had become addicted to entertaining people during our years on radio and in appearances, so they happily responded to invitations to sing at gatherings in the Orangeburg area.

On one of my visits to Orangeburg, Dad informed me that he and Mother had picked up another singer, and, calling themselves the Stumphole Trio, they had recorded four songs for Cee Bee, Low Country Music, Inc. Ever the enterprising, creative father, he named the three artists Oodus, Flossie, and Hezzie! I'm sure they sold their 45-inch disks all over the lower part of South Carolina. There were two songs on each side: "Sioux City Sue," "I'll Never Let You Cry" and "I Love You the Best of All," "Down the River of Golden Dreams."

Mother had a standard pose for pictures; the presence of any camera automatically brought out her stage smile. She had learned her social graces well from Pat Walker. She acquired lovely antique furniture, china, silver, and crystal for entertaining. She enjoyed sewing aprons, dish towels, napkins, and linens; she also made quilts and braided rugs from scraps of cloth. We children were given many of these. She loved "old-fashioned things," mostly of the colonial period, or objects having a "country look."

Mother dressed elegantly and appeared quite at home in any setting. With Betty she often sang duets and socialized with prominent people throughout the country. One of my favorite snapshots, taken in Florida, shows her standing next to Perry Como.

I was hardly prepared for the telephone call that came to the Eden parsonage on April 11, 1979, at four o'clock in the morning. On the other end of the line someone said, "Kenneth, I'm a paramedic in Orangeburg, South Carolina. I hate to tell you, but 'Ma' Johnson died about an hour ago."

Stunned for a moment, I asked if I could speak to my father. When Dad came to the phone, he explained how he had risen around three and put on a pot of coffee; Mother meandered into the kitchen/den a few minutes later to join him. "I poured her a cup of coffee and she sat down in her big chair to drink it. When I returned from the bathroom, her head was tilted to the back of the chair, and I knew she was dead. I called the paramedics, but there was nothing they could do. 'Ma' apparently died of a stroke."

I groped for words to reassure my father as well as myself. "I'll be down there later in the morning," I told him. Dad told me he would call Bob and Jim, and I agreed to call Betty. I shared the sad news with Evelyn and the children before making that call.

At about nine that morning the family loaded up to start the four-hour trip to Orangeburg. Shortly after we began, I asked Evelyn if she would mind driving. She took over the wheel, and I began scribbling some notes on a pad. I thought to myself, "What if *I* were conducting mother's service. What would I say?" I began to sketch out an order of service, thinking that I would offer to secure the bulletins. I then imagined myself making the remarks, believing that by training and experience I could do this better than anyone else, though not in the service.

When I met the supply pastor of First Presbyterian, Dr. Dean A. Bailey, that evening and learned that he planned only Scripture and prayers, I felt comfortable in sharing with him what had happened to me as I traveled to Orangeburg. He readily agreed to my arranging for the bulletin, adding, "I'd also like for you to give those remarks—if you think you can do it."

"Let me think about that overnight, and discuss it with Dad and my sister and brothers," I told the pastor. When I spoke to Dad and told him Dr. Bailey had asked me to assist in the service, he gave his blessing, as did my siblings. Betty volunteered to arrange the flowers for the service; Bob, Jim, and Dad agreed to make all the necessary funeral home arrangements; and they asked me to make plans for the service. I called Dr. Bailey and told him I would accept his invitation to assist in the service. We also invited the former pastor and a good friend of my parents, Dr. W. McLeod Frampton, Jr., to assist.

The service was held at First Presbyterian Church in Orangeburg, on Good Friday, April 13, 1979—two days before our daughter was to be married in Eden! The funeral service opened to the reassuring strains of "Be Still, My Soul." I sat with the family at the end of the pew, next to the outside aisle. As the organ played "The Old Rugged Cross," I glanced down the pew at my family members, recalling those glad times when we had recorded that hymn for Columbia Records.

After the Scripture readings by Dr. Frampton, I slipped up to the pulpit and shared this meditation with the congregation:

> This afternoon we have come together as a family—not in the reunion we had anticipated for this weekend, but as a community of faith that has embraced us in very special ways. Dad told us of your unusual hospitality when he first moved to Caw Caw Swamp twenty years ago. Mother would often tell us of the things you had done for her and Dad. Now more than ever our family is convinced of the breadth and depth of your friendship.
>
> Being the eldest of the children, perhaps I can speak a word about Mother that will help assuage the family's grief and, at the same time, provide you with a reminder of God's gifts through the life and witness of "Ma" Johnson—the real producer of the Johnson Family Singers, correctly referred to in today's *Charlotte Observer* as the "backbone" of the family!
>
> I can easily begin with mother's talents. They did not lead her to great fame or fortune but they did make an indelible impression upon our lives as well as the lives of others. Mother was a remarkable cook, especially in her younger days—when Jim and Bob and Betty and Dad and I would devour a baked hen or a fried rabbit in no time flat. Don't press me to name the biggest eaters in the family! Fondly, though, we remember Mother's work in the kitchen and can assure you that everything which Grady Cole said about her cooking in those Quaker Oats commercials was true!
>
> The older people here will better remember Mother as an alto singer. Here she also had obvious talent. She would sometimes sing the lead part with the grandchildren in the song "On Moonlight Bay"—but this was not her natural state of excellence. Mother's love of and gift for the alto part found its way into thousands of programs, broadcasts,

telecasts, and recordings. So when we now hear her rich and resonant voice sing "You've got to walk that long, lonesome road," it will take on added meaning.

Mother also possessed the gift of frugality. We kidded her a lot when the energy crisis came and she shifted from lights to candles and from electricity to fireplace—but she may have been more prophetic here than any of us will admit. President Carter would be proud of her energy conservation! In our consumption-oriented culture, we desperately need her example. If disposals could talk, they might have lots to say about *our* wastefulness—but not Mother's!

I could easily speak of other conservative habits—like gardening, canning, sewing, quilting, and saving. Dad will surely find money tucked away in drawers and in shoe boxes and under mattresses for years to come! Suffice it to say, we'll miss Mother's cash handouts and frequent presents.

Our mother was a thoughtful person. Cards and letters were standard practice for her, with addresses and spellings often bringing added color and charm! The circle of her concern may not have been wide enough, but who of us is satisfied with his circle of concern? Not many of us are like John Wesley, who claimed the world as his parish; nevertheless, to cover one's parish or one's family as Mother did is a notable achievement.

I marvel at what Mother did with those gifts which God gave her—the gifts of creativity in the kitchen, studio, and on stage—as well as the gifts of frugality and thoughtfulness. Were I to single out Mother's chief claim to fame, though, I would have to say it was her simple faith.

The religious quality of my mother's life was unique. She had her limitations, of course; she made her share of mistakes, like the rest of us. Even so, she possessed a faith that resulted in some uncanny insights and observations. No son or daughter or grandchild ever had a more devoted supporter. She looked at all of us through rose-colored glasses, commending our good points and overlooking our bad ones. People with degrees may have exceeded her in academics but they could hardly improve upon some of her diagnoses and remedies! Her parental counsel will not get out of date soon.

We were amazed at Mother's perceptions, which made her appear clairvoyant at times. For example, when she accepted the invitation of Dr. and Mrs. Grady Ballard to our daughter's wedding rehearsal dinner tomorrow night, she told me she had simply replied, "Thank you, Mrs. Ballard, for inviting us." When I reminded my mother that she might have been more specific in her acceptance note, she said, "That's what Pa told me I should have done." In retrospect, we now see that a father and son can both be wrong!

My dad and sister and brothers have their favorite family song. My favorite, "A Haven in Heaven," was written by our good friend Larry Walker. The text goes:

I'm gonna find me a haven in heaven
  where I can be happy all day.
I'm gonna rest by the River Jordan
  and let it wash my sins away.
I'm gonna join in the heavenly music
  and sing with the angels above
When I reach that haven in heaven,
  that beautiful haven of love.

Sentimental? Visionary? Perhaps. But this is Good Friday—a day in the church year when we recall the sacrifice of a Galilean Who counseled His disciples: " . . . I go to prepare a place for you. And if I go and prepare a place for you, I will come again, and receive you unto myself; that where I am, there ye may be also" (John 14: 2–3).

Following the pastoral prayer by Dr. Bailey, we sang, "O God, our help in ages past," and left the church to the organ strains of Karg Elert's "Now Thank We All Our God."

Family and friends reassembled at the Good Shepherd Mausoleum, where Dad had purchased two spaces a few years before. On several occasions I had commended him for this. Following the brief committal, we walked slowly away. "Brother," my sister told me, putting her arm around me, "the service was beautiful. Somehow we've got to package it for friends of Mother who couldn't attend." I knew what she meant.

When I returned to Orangeburg a few days later, I got copies of the prayers used by the other ministers and then invested some of the memorial gifts to reproduce the bulletin, containing all the elements of the service. One of my most therapeutic exercises was sitting down and writing notes to all the people I could identify, enclosing for them the bulletin. That little ivory bulletin consisted of eight pages, the last one quoting the tribute from Proverbs: "A good wife who can find? She is far more precious than jewels. The heart of her husband trusts in her, and he will have no lack of gain. She does him good, and not harm, all the days of her life . . . She looks well to the ways of her household, and does not eat the bread of idleness. Her children rise up and call her blessed . . ." (Proverbs 31: 10–12, 27–28b).

A FINAL SEPARATION

The remaining months of 1979 were not easy ones for Dad. We children visited him as often as possible, but the pain of Mother's death was obvious. When I tried to help him verbalize his grief, he would shrug his shoulders and say, "Son, you just want to continue your mother's life."

As a pastor, I had the advantage of a large support system. A month after Mother's death, I wrote to Dad: " . . . to date our church has received forty some memorial gifts—including one $500 gift to the Triad Home (that's our Methodist retirement home in Winston-Salem). I have received in addition some 70 sympathy cards and another 35 or so personal letters, 10 different floral tributes, and 15 families with food across the month. To each person I have given a copy of the service, along with a personal note of appreciation."

On August 24, I made a special trip to Orangeburg to see my father. Both of us, I felt, needed support. My first stop was at the Good Shepherd Mausoleum, where I stood for a few minutes in silence, cried, and made an audible prayer for Mother and Dad.

When I arrived at Dad's house, he invited me in and asked if I would join him for a cup of coffee. We sat down at the kitchen table and for the next six hours had an extensive interview, which I recorded on his cassette player. I explained that for some time I had wanted him to share with me more details of his early life—as far back as he could remember up until he married Mother in 1924. The information he shared with me forms the basis of his story in the first chapter.

My father seemed to recede into his shell more and more, not writing or calling. I knew he was suffering the pangs of grief. His fifty-five-year marriage to Mother had produced a closeness despite their various separations. As a pastor, I knew that the death of a loved one produces grief in proportion to one's investment in a life. I do not believe Dad was aware of his investment in Mother's life until she was gone. Unfortunately, he had little or no experience with grief and was unable to handle it properly. He had the mistaken notion that the less said about it, the better. I knew this approach would bother him sooner or later.

A shocking moment came in a matter-of-fact telephone call from him in February of 1980, when he told of his plans to marry a twice-widowed woman from St. George named Margaret Knight. He mentioned that he and Mother had once met her at some social. Unlike Mother, Margaret was no singer. From a later conversation I had with her, I gathered that she had pursued Dad with sweet talk and cooking after Mother died. In effect, Dad told me he was marrying her because of his loneliness. It seemed to me that a second marriage was a poor way of handling one's grief!

On February 19, like a dutiful son, I wrote to Margaret welcoming her into the family: "I shall expect you to be your own person, Margaret—which means that you don't have to fill any shoes! Mother made her contribution to our family; it was important and is lovingly remembered. You will make yours—not as an imitator but as a unique and different person, with your own set of gifts and achievements. Comparisons may be inevitable but they are hardly divine! My goal is to be open and accepting of you as you are."

Before his marriage to Margaret on April 19, Dad had talked about the need for updating his will. I was delighted to learn that he had gone ahead and signed a prenuptial agreement with Margaret, one which provided that, at her death, all of her premarital assets would go to her children, and any assets which Dad brought into the marriage would be given to us children at the time of his death. I commended Dad on his farsightedness and agreed to his request to go to Orangeburg in May to explain his new will to Margaret and her daughter, Jackie, and to receive from him an updated general power of attorney.

Later my father changed his will, making greater provisions for Margaret and leaving to her most of the family assets. Less than six months after his marriage, he ended up having major surgery in what today is the Carolinas Regional Medical Center in Charlotte. The doctors successfully removed an aneurism from his chest. While this condition had undoubtedly existed for some time, I believe Dad's difficulty in expressing grief aggravated the condition.

After discussing Dad's case with the doctor, I tried to persuade my father to forego the use of tobacco, explaining that I had been told that his lungs were coated with a black film. He seemed to appreciate this information, but it did not cause him to give up smoking. "I've lived a pretty long life so far," he responded.

"Maybe I have a few more years." This was his polite way of saying, "Thanks, son, but no thanks!"

Unfortunately my brothers and I visited Dad less frequently in Orangeburg. He had given up letter writing before Mother's death, due to arthritis in his hands. We were dependent upon Margaret for information about him, and it was sparse indeed. For example, when Dad suffered a stroke in April 1987, we were not informed about it until June! When we found out, Bob and I drove down from Charlotte to see him.

We found that the stroke had caused Dad's face to be drawn to one side, but that he was continuing his WDIX announcing with little interruption. "How do you read the commercials?" I asked. In typical Johnson fashion, he responded, "I just take my handkerchief"—he reached into his back pocket to demonstrate—"and wipe . . . and go on!" Dad was determined not to let handicaps deter him from the life he loved, which meant broadcasting and entertaining people.

While riding back to Charlotte with my brother, I told him I planned to record a special tribute and send it to Dad, so that he could play it on his radio program. I arranged to make a cassette immediately when I got back to Winston-Salem. When he got the tape, Dad promptly played it on one of his programs. Here is the text of "A Tribute to Dad":

Hi, Dad! I want to talk with you for a few minutes and share a surprise. So, if you're listening at home, please turn off the TV and rest yourself in the big chair, and listen. Ever since my visit with you on July 3, 1987, I have wanted to prepare this message for you—a message which I believe you and your WDIX listeners may find interesting.

Dad, I want you to know that I love you and appreciate the gifts and graces which are uniquely yours. If I had to list four attributes which I admire in you—four qualities which have helped to shape my life—I would have to say, first of all, that you are an affable father. You are approachable, easy to speak to, mild, gentle, and amiable. Your many listeners are aware of this. So are your sponsors, some of whom have stuck with you for more than thirty years! Your warm, inviting personality is one that attracts and makes people feel included and at ease—over the radio and everywhere else. This trait, unconsciously developed by you, is one which came with your packaging at birth! Some credit must also go to "Granny Johnson" and "Uncle Jack," who raised you.

You are also an ingenious dad. You come as near as anybody I know who can sell refrigerators to Eskimos! Remember your one-man ad campaigns for church hymnals back in the 1930s? You also didn't do badly with gas rationing during World War II when gift-rabbits helped to woo and win support for extra gallons! The family is also aware of the rabbit gifts to Jess Willard and others at WBT—gifts which helped to launch our radio-singing career. Most remarkable of all, perhaps, was your ingenious trip into the radio control room in the early 1950s, where you quickly mastered the buttons and switches and became an announcer! The rest is history. Your inventiveness, originality, resourcefulness and cleverness—including your several elections as "Mayor of Caw Caw Swamp"—will not only follow you all the days of your life but have lodged in your children and your children's children!

Third, you are a persevering dad. With you, handicaps need not handicap! We still chuckle about those conversations when people would ask you, "Pa, which was your college?" You would respond, "I went through Elon!" You could say this without cracking a smile because, indeed, we did have to travel through Elon College to get from Greensboro to our little pine log cabin near Burlington! You also showed the family how to stick together during tough times—times when bookings were low and radio shows were canceled. Remember the summer when you and I supplemented the family income by working on a thrashing machine? As the "family secretary," I can cite other difficult chapters and verses which you overcame.

I said at the beginning that I had four virtues which I wanted you to hear about as you sit there in your easy chair. You are not only an affable, ingenious and persevering father, but you will always stand out in my memory for your confident manner. You exude an assured air without being cocky. Long before Norman Vincent Peale and Robert Schuller popularized positive thinking, you were practicing it—letting your children know that a positive attitude is the name of the game. Some of us have also learned from you that the positive is what motivates people. We shall always be grateful to you for this important lesson in living.

Now, Dad, if you're still awake (!), I want to share with you a song which I first heard you and Mother sing when I was eight or nine years old. The Auctioneers, a barbershop chorus which rehearses at Burkhead Church on Monday nights, gave me the privilege of directing them in this number on July 6, 1987. I lovingly dedicate it to you and to the blessed memory of Mother.

I then directed the Auctioneers Chorus of around a hundred voices in their close-harmony rendition of Joe Goodwin and Larry Shay's song:

> Tie me to your apron strings again—
> I know there's room for me upon your knee.
> Bring back all those happy hours when
> you kissed my tears away from day to day.

I thought that I was right, but I was wrong,
> Please take me back tonight where I belong.
Sing a cradle song to me and then
> Won't you tie me to your apron strings again?[1]

Three or four weeks later, Dad called to thank me for the tape, telling me how his listeners had enjoyed it. "I plan to use it again next Father's Day," he told me. Unfortunately, he had to give up his work in August of the following year because of ill health. Two weeks before his death he called, asking, "Son, would you please send me another copy of that tape? I misplaced the one you sent me. . . . I want a friend to hear it." Happily Frank Watson at the local radio station in Shelby was able to record another copy, which I mailed to my father.

In April of 1989, Evelyn and I and our son Wesley had stopped by to visit with Dad at the trailer near St. George where he had moved. Within a month of that visit, he suffered a heart attack. Again, the word of his hospitalization was delayed in reaching us; we heard on a Saturday night around ten o'clock, and I went to see him the next day after the worship service at the church I was serving in Shelby, North Carolina. Two weeks later, on May 16, 1989, he had a second heart attack and died. The doctor called to give me the message.

Dad died on a Tuesday. On the Sunday preceding his death, we had attended the graduation of our youngest son, Christopher, from Appalachian State University in Boone. Wesley, who had been delayed in finishing his college work, was set to graduate from New York University on Thursday of the same week. Instead of going to Wesley's graduation, family members gathered on Friday in Orangeburg for Dad's funeral.

After the service, we made our way to the Good Shepherd Mausoleum, where Dad's body was entombed in a crypt next to Mother. After the benediction, Bob and Jim joined me spontaneously in singing quietly:

Precious mem'ries, unseen angels,
> Sent from somewhere to my soul;
How they linger, ever near me,
> And the sacred past unfold.

---

[1]"Tie Me to Your Apron Strongs Again." Words and music by Joe Goodwin and Larry Shay. © 1925 by MCA Music Publishing, a division of Universal Studios, Inc. Copyright renewed. International copyright secured. All rights reserved.

Precious mem'ries, how they linger,
How they ever flood my soul,
In the stillness of the midnight,
Precious, sacred scenes unfold.[2]

So that the graves could be more accessible to the children and grandchildren, my parents' remains were transferred to the Pleasant Grove Memorial Park in Charlotte in December of 1996. Their bodies rest there in peace, in graves which Dad had purchased in 1962 and almost within sight of the house that we had lived in twenty years earlier.

In the stillness of the midnight,
Precious, sacred scenes unfold.

DISCOGRAPHY

In most sessions, only singles were made. Our final RCA-Victor session, which produced LPM–2126, was an exception. The vintage Johnson sound disappears from voices as well as from instrumentation in the fourth Columbia session. To our dismay, Art Satherly pushed the "country sound" in these records, as well as in the ones that followed in session five. The Columbia records from our first session in 1946 contain a more youthful sound than the RCA-Victor album produced in our final session in 1959. Betty, only seventeen in the first session, was thirty in the final one. Betty's Columbia records parallel and relate to the family's, so they are included here. She went on to record for RCA-Victor and several other labels.

The matrix number (order of the recording) is listed to the left of the title. The record number is given to the right of the names of writers/composers, in parenthesis.

COLUMBIA RECORDS

Session 1   Charlotte, NC — September 27, 1946

Vocalists: Pa, Ma, Red, Betty, Bob, and Jim
Instrumentalists: "Pa" Johnson, guitar; Larry Walker, piano

CCO–4679	Sunday Morning in Dixie (Walker)	Col 37340, 20118
CCO–4680	A House Built on a Rock (Rose)	Col 38087, 20405
CCO–4681	He Put the Sunshine in My Soul (Dexter)	Col 37340, 20118
CCO–4682	Lord, Build Me a Cabin in Glory (Stewart)	Col 38087, 20405

Session 2   Charlotte, NC — October 20, 1946

Vocalists: Pa, Ma, Red, Betty, Bob, and Jim
Instrumentalists: "Pa" Johnson, guitar; Larry Walker, piano

CCO–4675	I'll Reap My Harvest in Heaven (Jenkins)	Col 37225, 20098
CCO–4676	The Old Family Bible (Meadows – Darling)	Col 37887, 20369
CCO–4677	Wait for the Light to Shine (Rose)	Col 37887, 20369
CCO–4678	Cabin in the Valley of the Pines (Brumley)	Col 37225, 20098

Session 3   Nashville, TN — December 28, 1947

Vocalists: Pa, Ma, Red, Betty, Bob, and Jim
Instrumentalists: "Pa" Johnson, guitar; Larry Walker, piano

CO–38753	Just Say a Little Prayer (Dexter)	Col 20471
CO–38754	I've Got a Feeling ("Ma" Johnson)	Col 20536
CO–38755	Keep on the Sunny Side (Carter – Garett)	Col 20509
CO–38756	A Haven in Heaven (Walker)	Col 20471
CO–38762	May the Circle Be Complete (Fowler – Hall)	Col 20426
CO–38763	Somebody's Waiting for Me ("Pa" Johnson)	Col 20426
CO–38764	Just Like Me (Rose)	Col 20509
CO–38765	There's a Little Pine Log Cabin (Brumley)	Col 20536

Session 4   Charlotte, NC — May 4, 1949

Vocalists: Pa, Ma, Red, Betty, Bob and Jim
Instrumentalists: Arthur Smith, fiddle; Nat Richardson, steel guitar; Sonny Smith, rhythm guitar

CO–40754	God is My Landlord (Kirby)	Col 20603
CO–40755	Let's Ride That Plane (Fowler)	Col 20603
CO–40756	The Old Country Church ("Pa" Johnson)	Col 20653
CO–40757	When It's Starlight on the Bluegrass (Vier)	Col 20589
CO–40758	Grandma's Spinning Wheel ("Pa" Johnson)	Col 20589
CO–40759	You've Got to Walk That Lonesome Road (Brumley)	Col 20693
CO–40760	It's an Unfriendly World to Me (Brumley)	Col 20693
CO–40761	I'll Meet You in the Morning (Brumley)	Col 20653

Session 5   New York, NY — June 23, 1950

Vocalists: Pa, Ma, Red, Betty, Bob, and Jim
Instrumentalists: "Pa" Johnson, Ray Smith, Roy Horton

CO–43990	He Will Pay All the Cost ("Pa" Johnson)	Col 20767
CO–43991	Reunion in the Sky ("Pa" Johnson)	Col 20759
CO–43992	Get On Your Knees, Sinner (Smith – Jenkins)	Col 20736

CO–43993	I Have Got Old-Time Religion (Bob and Jim Johnson)	Col 20759
CO–43994	The Hallelujah Train (Smith – Jenkins)	Col 20736
CO–43995	Don't Be Ashamed of Your Religion (Connors – Smith)	Col 20767

Session 6   Nashville, TN — May 7, 1951

Vocalists: Pa, Ma, Red, Betty, Bob, and Jim
Instrumentalist: "Pa" Johnson, guitar

CO–45880	Deliverance Will Come (Matthias)	Col 20934
CO–45881	Farther Along (Stevens – Baxter)	Col 20867
CO–45882	Old-Fashioned Cottage in Heaven ("Pa" Johnson)	Col 20934
CO–45883	The Death of Ellenton ("Pa" Johnson – D. Smith)	Col 20895
CO–45884	Precious Memories (Wright)	Col 20838
CO–45885	Come And See Me (Presley)	Col 20895
CO–45886	The Old Rugged Cross (Bennard)	Col 20867
CO–45887	I Like the Old-Time Way ("Pa" Johnson)	Col 20838

Session 7   Nashville, TN — June 13, 1952

Vocalists: Pa, Ma, Red, Betty, Bob, and Jim
Instrumentalist: "Pa" Johnson, guitar

CO–48048	The Haven of Rest (Gilmour – Moore)	Col 21069
CO–48049	Are You Washed in the Blood? (Hoffman)	Col 21069
CO–48050	Pass Me Not (Crosby – Doane)	Col 21126
CO–48051	I Need the Prayers (Vaughan)	Col 21126
CO–48052	Where No Cabins Fall (Jeffress)	Col 20991
CO–48053	Room for My Savior Today (Harrington)	Col 20991
CO–48054	Bright Mansions Above (Heidelberg)	Col 21050
CO–48055	Faith of Our Fathers (Faber – Hemy)	Col 21050

Session 8   New York, NY — September 4, 1953

Vocalists: Pa, Ma, Red, Betty, Bob, and Jim
Instrumentalist: "Pa" Johnson, guitar

CO–49931	Whispering Hope (Hawthorne)	Col 21180
CO–49932	The Sweetest Gift (Coats)	Col 21180
CO–49933	The Old Family Circle (Trent – Walker)	Col 21251
CO–49934	I'd Like to Feel at Home (Wells, Smith)	Col 21251
CO–49935	My Home, Sweet Home (Vandall)	Col 21308
CO–49936	His Love is Mine (Baxter – Stafford)	Col 21308

COLUMBIA RECORDS BY BETTY JOHNSON

Session I   Nashville, TN — May 9, 1951

Vocalist: Betty Johnson
Instrumentalists: Marvin Hughes, organ; Grady Martin, guitar; Bob Moore, bass

CO–45910	An Evening Prayer (Battersby – Gabriel)	Col 20834
CO–45911	Oh Gentle Shepherd (Walker)	Col 20834

Session 2   Nashville, TN — September 24, 1951

Vocalist: Betty Johnson
Instrumentalists: Marvin Hughes, organ; Grady Martin, guitar; Bob Moore, bass

CO–46933	My Mother's Prayer (Nolan – Kerr)	Col 20882
CO–46934	When the Savior Reached Down for Me (Wright)	Col 20919
CO–46935	A Promise And a Prayer (Nolan – Kerr)	Col 20882
CO–46936	Pray for Me (Leibert)	Col 20919

Session 3   Nashville, TN — June 13, 1952

Vocalist: Betty Johnson; backup vocals: Pa, Ma, Red, Bob, and Jim
Instrumentalists: Marvin Hughes, organ; Grady Martin, guitar; Bob Moore, bass

CO–48056	My Mother's Bible (Altman – Manning)	Col 21024
CO–48057	What a Friend We Have in Jesus (Scriven – Converse)	Col 20984
CO–48058	Have Thine Own Way, Lord (Pollard – Stebbins)	Col 20984
CO–48059	Where He Leads Me (Blandly, Norris)	Col 21024

SPECIAL COLUMBIA ISSUES AND ALBUMS

45–EP, B–11771

Faith of Our Fathers (Family)
What a Friend (Betty)
The Old Rugged Cross (Family)
Are You Washed in the Blood? (Family)

45–EP, B–1172, Vol. 2

Oh Gentle Shepherd (Betty)
Farther Along (Family)
Whispering Hope (Family)
Have Thine Own Way, Lord (Family)

45–RPM (Hall of Fame Series), 4–54032–s

Farther Along
The Old Rugged Cross

ALBUMS

Faith of Our Fathers, CL 1177

Faith of Our Fathers (Family)
What a Friend We Have in Jesus (Betty)
The Old Rugged Cross (Family)
Are You Washed in the Blood? (Family)
Oh Gentle Shepherd (Betty)
Farther Along (Family)

Whispering Hope (Family)
Have Thine Own Way, Lord (Betty)
The Haven of Rest (Family)
Precious Memories (Family)
Where He Leads Me (Betty)
An Evening Prayer (Betty)

Betty Johnson: An Evening Prayer, HL 7303

An Evening Prayer
Oh Gentle Shepherd
My Mother's Prayer
When the Savior Reached Down for Me
A Promise and a Prayer

Pray For Me
My Mother's Bible
What a Friend We Have in Jesus
Have Thine Own Way, Lord
Where He Leads Me

Library of Congress, LCM 2095

Songs of Local History and Events (Folk Music in America, Volume 12)

This album contains songs by 15 different artists/groups, including The Johnson Family Singers and featuring a song recorded by them on Columbia Records in Session 6, on May 7, 1951:

The Death of Ellenton

COED RECORDS BY THE JOHNSON FAMILY SINGERS

Session 1   New York, NY — c. 1960

Vocalists: Pa, Ma, Betty, Bob, and Jim
Instrumentalists: Charles Grean,leader-bass; unknown guitar; unknown organ; unknown drums

L805–6817   There's a Star-Spangled Banner Waving Somewhere
    (Roberts – Darnell – Dave)   COED 532
L80W–6818   Take a Little Look in the Good Book (Grean)   COED 532

RCA-VICTOR RECORDS BY THE JOHNSON FAMILY SINGERS

Session 1   Nashville, TN — September 21, 1954

Vocalists: Pa, Ma, Betty, Bob, and Jim
Instrumentalists: Charles Grean, leader-bass; Jack Shook, rhythm guitar; Chet Atkins, electric guitar;
   Marvin Hughes, reed organ and piano
Producer: Steve Sholes

E4VW–5501   Speak to Him (Coben)   RCA 47–6047
E4VB–5502   Do You Know Where God Lives? (Coben)   RCA 20–5910
E4VB–5503   The Lord is Counting on You (Hamblen)   RCA 20–5910
E4VW–5504   He Had to Go to Calvary (Moody)   RCA 47–6582

Session 2   Nashville, TN — January 16–17, 1955

Vocalists: Pa, Ma, Betty, Bob, and Jim
Instrumentalists: Charles Grean, leader-bass; Chet Atkins, electric guitar; John Gordy, piano and organ;
   Jack Shook, rhythm guitar; Jerry Byrd, steel guitar
Producer: Steve Sholes

F2WW–0208   Let Me Stay a Little Longer (Grean – Hicks – Frame)   RCA 47–6114
F2WW–0209   And He Was There (Coben)   RCA 47–6372
F2WW–0214   You Must Be Born Again (Hamblen)   RCA 47–6114
F2WW–0215   Climbing Up the Ladder (Johnson – Grean)   RCA 47–6047

Session 3   Nashville, TN — May 27–29, 1955

Vocalists: Pa, Ma, Bob, and Jim
Instrumentalists: Charles Grean, leader-bass; Chet Atkins, electric guitar; Marvin Hughes, piano and
   organ
Producer: Steve Sholes

F2WW–2284   When We All Get to Heaven (Hewitt – Wilson)   RCA 547–0691

F2WW–2285	When the Roll is Called Up Yonder (Black)	RCA 547–0690
F2WW–2286	Shall We Gather at the River? (Lowery – Grean)	RCA 547–0691
F2WW–2287	Standing on the Promises (Carter)	RCA LPM–1128

Vocalists: Pa, Ma, Betty, Bob, and Jim
Instrumentalists: Charles Grean, leader-bass; Chet Atkins, electric guitar; Marvin Hughes, piano and
    organ
Producer: Steve Sholes

F2WW–2291	Tell Me the Old, Old Story (Hankey – Deans)	RCA 47–6912
F2WW–2292	Stand Up, Stand Up for Jesus (Duffield – Webb)	RCA 547–0690
F2WW–2293	I Will Sing the Wondrous Story (Rowley – Dilhorn)	RCA 547–0691
F2WW–2294	Campin' in Canaan's Land (Bartlett)	RCA LPM–1128

Vocalists: Pa, Ma, Betty, Bob, and Jim
Instrumentalists: Charles Grean, leader-bass; Marvin Hughes, piano; Chet Atkins, electric guitar; Dale
    Parker, banjo; Farris Courcey, drums
Producer: Steve Sholes

F2WW–2295	Your First Day in Heaven (Hamblen)	RCA 47–6372
F2WW–2296	Old-Time Religion (Arr. Grean)	RCA 547–0690
F2WW–2297	Standin' in the Need of Prayer (Traditional)	RCA 547–0690
F2WW–2298	Keep on the Sunny Side of Life (Carter – Garett)	RCA LPM–1128

Session 4   Chicago, Ill — August 17, 1955

Vocalist: "Pa" Johnson
Instrumentalists: Homer Haynes, leader-guitar; Jethro Burns, mandolin; John Frigo, bass; Marty
    Rubenstein, piano; Frank Rullo, drums
Producer: Not listed

| F2WW–0754 | Shifting, Whispering Sands (I) (Gilbert – Gilbert) | RCA 47–6243 |
| F2WW–0755 | Shifting, Whispering Sands (II) (Gilbert – Gilbert) | RCA 47–6243 |

Session 5   Nashville, TN — November 11, 1956

Vocalists: "Pa" Johnson, Betty Johnson, Betty Dillard, Wm. G. Wright, Jr.
Instrumentalists: Chet Atkins, leader-electric guitar; Loren Otis Shook, guitar; Marvin Hughes, organ and
    piano; bass, Bob L. Moore
Producer: Steve Sholes

G2WB–5413	Precious Memories (Wright)	RCA 20–6912
G2WW–5414	May God Be With You (Cury – Maupin)	RCA 47–6756
G2WW–5415	You Take Your Road (Lowe)	RCA 47–6756

Session 6   Nashville, TN — June 29, 1959

Vocalists: Pa, Ma, Red, Betty, Bob, and Jim; unknown backup vocalists
Instrumentalists: Marvin Hughes, organ; John Gordy, piano
Producer: Charles Grean

K2WB–0578	Stand Up, Stand Up for Jesus (Duffield – Webb)	RCA LPM–2126
K2WB–0579	What a Friend We Have in Jesus (Scriven – Converse)	RCA LPM–2126
K2WB–0580	Softly and Tenderly Jesus is Calling (Thompson)	RCA LPM–2126
K2WB–0581	Crown Him With Many Crowns (Bridges – Elvey)	RCA LPM–2126
K2WB–0582	I Love to Tell the Story (Hankey – Fischer)	RCA LPM–2126
K2WB–0583	Rock of Ages, Cleft for Me (Toplady – Hastings)	RCA LPM–2126
K2WB–0584	He Leadeth Me (Gilmore – Bradbury)	RCA LPM–2126
K2WB–0585	Now the Day is Over (Baring – Gould – Barnby)	RCA LPM–2126
K2WB–0586	Holy, Holy, Holy (Heber – Dykes)	RCA LPM–2126
K2WB–0587	Near the Cross (Crosby – Doane)	RCA LPM–2126
K2WB–0588	Shall We Gather at the River (Lowry)	RCA LPM–2126
K2WB–0589	Blest Be the Tie That Binds (Fawcett – Naegeli)	RCA LPM–2126
K2WB–0590	I Am Thine, O Lord (Crosby – Doane)	RCA LPM–2126
K2WB–0591	Tell Me the Old, Old Story (Hankey – Doane)	RCA LPM–2126
K2WB–0592	Just as I Am (Elliott – Bradbury)	RCA LPM–2126
K2WB–0593	God Be With You (Rankin – Tomer)	RCA LPM–2126

OTHER FAMILY ALBUMS

Old Time Religion, LPM–1128

Old-Time Religion
Stand Up, Stand Up for Jesus
When We All Get to Heaven
I Will Sing the Wondrous Story
Keep on the Sunny Side of Life
He Had to Go to Calvary

Shall We Gather at the River
Tell Me the Old, Old Story
When the Roll is Called Up Yonder
Standin' in the Need of Prayer
Campin' in Canaan's Land
Standing on the Promises

Old Time Religion, 45EP, EPB–1128

Old-Time Religion
Stand Up, Stand Up for Jesus
When We All Get to Heaven
I Will Sing the Wondrous Story
Shall We Gather at the River
Tell Me the Old, Old Story
When the Roll is Called Up Yonder
Standin' in the Need of Prayer

Old-Time Family Religion, CAL–816(e)

The "family groups" are on this album, each group with four selections. The first track features
The Johnson Family Singers:

Old-Time Religion
Standin' in the Need of Prayer
Tell Me the Old, Old Story
When the Roll is Called Up Yonder

The second track features The Speer Family; the third track, The Carter Family.

Share Your Favorite Hymns With The Johnson Family, CAL–952

Shall We Gather at the River
Shifting, Whispering Sands
You Must Be Born Again
Keep on the Sunny Side of Life
Standing on the Promises

Precious Memories
I Will Sing the Wondrous Story
May God Be With You
Stand Up, Stand Up for Jesus
When We All Get to Heaven

Sing Hymns With The Johnson Family Singers, LPM–2126

Stand Up, Stand Up for Jesus
What a Friend We Have in Jesus
Softly and Tenderly
Crown Him With Many Crowns
I Love to Tell the Story

Rock of Ages
He Leadeth Me
Now the Day is Over

Holy, Holy, Holy
Near the Cross
Shall We Gather at the River
Blest Be the Tie
I Am Thine, O Lord
Tell Me the Old, Old Story
Just As I Am
God Be With You

Reader's Digest 50 Beloved Songs of Faith, BMR3–101 (Record 2)

As the name implies, these three records features 50 different artists/groups. The second record in this three-part series features The Johnson Family Singers:

Standing on the Promises

CEE BEE RECORDS BY "MA" AND "PA" JOHNSON

Session 1   Hampton, SC — c. 1975

Vocalists: "Ma" & "Pa" Johnson, Wallace Shuler ["The Stumphole Trio"]
Instrumentalist: Lee Judy, guitar

Unknown	Sioux City Sue (Freedman – Thomas)	EP–1001–A
Unknown	I'll Never Let You Cry (Mitchell – Pollack)	EP–1001–A
Unknown	I Love You Best of All (Charlie/Ira Louvin)	EP–1001–B
Unknown	Down the River of Golden Dreams (Klenner/Shilkret)	EP–1001–B

RADIO TRANSCRIPTIONS

One of my prized possessions from our singing days is a collection of sixteen-inch radio transcriptions. I carted them about for years before acquiring a DuKane Micromatic machine on which to play them! The first group of transcriptions was given to me by the WBT record librarian, Bobbie Rierson; my brother Bob helped me to obtain others, especially those featuring the family. During the golden days of radio, there were no reel-to-reel tapes, cassettes, compact discs, or digital audio tapes; rather, radio stations used the transcription, which was usually acetate or vinyl. Some were made of glass and were quite fragile. A big spurt forward in the use of transcriptions came during World War II, when the U. S. government supplied them to the Armed Forces Radio Network to be broadcast to GIs around the world.

During our days in radio, I observed several uses for the transcription. Inasmuch as stations usually had only one large studio, programs were transcribed by one group in order to free up the studio for another. If a conflict in programming and/or personal schedules occurred, artists and/or stations sometimes transcribed programs for their own convenience. The transcription provided the station with an inexpensive way to repeat its programs, as can be seen in the dates for several of our transcriptions; also, it served as a backup if the artist could not appear because of sickness or some other emergency. Syndication was perhaps the most important reason for transcriptions. In the instance of our Quaker Oats shows, nos. 27–32, we recorded them on unknown dates at WBT during 1950–51; they were then shipped to various stations to be broadcast at different times. Sometimes programs were produced and sold to other stations, with spots left open for local commercials. In order to keep the listener from thinking that a program was "live," the announcer would begin by saying, "The following program is electrically transcribed . . ." and would conclude by saying, "The preceding program was electrically transcribed. . . ."

Following is a list of forty different programs. Numbering was done arbitrarily by the author, generally in chronological order. There was no consistent listing of names of programs in newspaper radio schedules. Sometimes a name is given, e.g., *Down Home with the Johnson Family Singers*, but a program was usually identified by the sponsor's name. Announcers were often as well known as the artist(s). Staff announcers for the station, they were assigned by management to the various programs. Because of their importance to a program's success, I have listed their names after the initial program title.

There was a definite evolution in "the Johnson sound." My twin brothers were only nine years old when we started singing on WBT; when we did our final program in 1951, they were twenty. The maturing of their voices, as well as of the voices of their older sister and brother, is easily detected in the transcriptions and family CD.

The addition of secular songs to our repertoire shows the direct influence of Larry Walker, the accomplished pianist (and announcer) on many of our records and programs. When Larry taught us a secular song, he would simply hand us the lyrics, sing the song for us, and then have us sing it with him. The harmony would fall into place, naturally and spontaneously. I do not recall ever seeing any sheet music or songbooks; thus, the listing of titles of songs on these transcriptions depends upon my recollection of what "Uncle Larry" called them or my discernment based upon a repeated line or phrase. Variation in titles seems to be much greater with songs than with books.

	Song	Artist
1. *Johnson Family Singers* (Announcer: Larry Walker) CBS 07-25-45, 4:45 P.M.	Sweetheart of All My Dreams I'm Gonna Take a Ride I Can't Give You Anything but Love In the Shadow of the Cross Sweet Sue	Family/Larry Family Larry Family Family/Larry
2. *Johnson Family Singers* CBS 07-30-45, 4:45 P.M.	Apple-Blossom Time The Old Gospel Ship Rosemary Precious Memories When You Wore a Tulip	Family/Larry Family Family/Larry Family Family/Larry

3. *BC Hymn Time* (Announcer: Lee Kirby) WBT 08-24-47, 1:05 P.M. 11-28-48, 1:05 P.M.	I Feel Like Traveling On How Beautiful Heaven Must Be He Loves Me So	Family Family Family
4. *BC Hymn Time* WBT 08-31-47 1:05 P.M.	Won't It Be Wonderful There If I Could Hear My Mother Pray Again Bright Mansions Above	Family Family Family
5. *BC Hymn Time* WBT 11-02-47, 1:05 P.M.	Showers of Blessings Dip Your Soul in God's Sunshine Are You Washed in the Blood?	Family Family Family
6. *BC Hymn Time* WBT 11-14-48, 1:05 P.M.	I'll Meet You in the Morning Just a Little Talk with Jesus The Haven of Rest	Family Family Family
7. *BC Hymn Time* WBT 11-28-48, 1:05 P.M.	Leaning on the Everlasting Arms Life's Evening Sun When I Take My Vacation in Heaven	Family Family Family
8. *BC Hymn Time* WBT 04-??-48, 1:05 P.M.	Standing on the Promises I Would Like to Go Back How Wonderful Heaven Must Be	Family Family Family
9. *BC Hymn Time* (inside out) WBT 09-13-49, 1:05 P.M. 03-12-50, 1:05 P.M.	The Land of the Unsetting Sun Just to Know Him Is to Love Him At Evening	Family Family Family
10. *BC Hymn Time* (inside out) WBT 11-20-49, 1:05 P.M. 03-26-50, 1:05 P.M.	Are You Washed in the Blood? Where Is My Wandering Boy Tonight? Sweet Hour of Prayer	Family Family Family
11. *BC Hymn Time* (inside out) WBT 11-27-49, 1:05 P.M. 03-26-50, 1:05 P.M.	The Lord Is There We Are Going Down the Valley Jesus Is Living in Me	Family Family Family
12. *BC Program* (outside band) (Announcer: Larry Walker) WBT ??-??-45, 5:35 P.M.	When You Wore a Tulip Did You Ever Get That Feeling in the Moonlight? Where Could I Go?	Family/Larry Betty/Larry Family

13. *BC Program*	Let Me Call You Sweetheart	Family/Larry
WBT	Just Around the Corner	Betty/Larry
11-01-47, 5:35 P.M.	Where We'll Never Grow Old	Family/Larry

14. *BC Program* (inside out)	When the White Azaleas Start	
WBT	Blooming	Family/Larry
12-20-47, 5:35 P.M.	When the Red, Red Robin Comes	
	Bob, Bob, Bobbing Along	Family/Larry
	A Shut-in's Prayer	Family

15. *BC Program* (inside out)	I've Got a Feeling	Family/Larry
WBT	Nice Work If You Can Get It	Betty/Larry
06-01-48, 5:35 P.M.	Heartbreaker	Family/Larry

16. *BC Program* (inside out)	It's a Good Day	Family/Larry
WBT	I'm Jealous of the One I Love	Betty/Larry
06-02-48, 5:35 P.M.	Grandfather's Clock	Family/Larry

17. *BC Program* (inside out, first	How Do You Do?	Family/Larry
band)	Silver Threads Among the Gold	Family/Larry
WBT	Keep on the Sunny Side (second band)	Family
01-03-49, 5:35 P.M.		
05-04-49		

18. *BC Program* (inside out)	Someday	Family/Larry
WBT	Put On Your Old Gray Bonnet	Family/Larry
08-12-49, 5:35 P.M.	He Said If I Be Lifted Up	Family
11-25-49		

19. *BC Program* (inside out)	If I Had My Way	Family/Larry
WBT	Up a Lazy River	Family/Larry
09-07-49, 5:35 P.M.	I've Been Listening in on Heaven	Family
02-04-50		

20. *BC Program* (inside out)	Just a Song at Twilight	Family/Larry
WBT	When We're Alone	Betty/Larry
09-08-49, 5:35 P.M.	Give the World a Song	Family
02-04-50		

21. *BC Program*	A Smile Goes a Long, Long Way	Family/Larry
WBT	Sunday Morning in Dixie	Family
03-??-50, 5:35 P.M.	Holy Be Thy Name	Family

22. *BC Program*	Side By Side	Family
WBT	Million Dollar Baby	Betty/Larry
03-24-50, 5:35 P.M.	God Shall Wipe Away All Tears	Family

23. *Down Home With . . .* (inside
    out)
    (Announcer: J. B. Clark)
    CBS
    04-14-45, 11:30 P.M.

We Will Stand By the Red, White and		
Blue	Family
Farther Along	Family
Hand in Hand with Jesus	Family
The Old Rugged Cross	Family
No Tears in Heaven	Family

24. *Down Home With . . .*
    CBS
    04-15-45, 8:45 A.M.

In the Shadow of the Cross	Family
Softly and Tenderly	Family
Precious Memories	Family
I'll Meet You in the Morning	Family
Tomorrow May Mean Goodbye	Family

25–A. *Fun by the Fireside, I*
    (Announcer: Fletcher
    Austin)
    WBT
    12-07-48 P.M.
    first 16:05 minutes

Alabamy Bound	Family/Larry
My Darling	Betty
A Little Bit of Ireland	Danny
Estrellita	Pat
Instrumental medley: piano, organ,	
guitar	

25–B. *Fun by the Fireside, II*
    (inside out)
    WBT
    12-07-48 P.M.
    last 12:31 minutes

Far Away Places	Family/Larry
Margie	Family/Larry
Peggy O'Neal	Danny
Oh, Johnny!	Betty
Linda	Clarence
Sweet Georgia Brown (instrumental)	Arthur
Just My Bill	Pat/Larry
Sweet Sue	Larry
For It Was Mary	Family/Larry

26–A. *Fun by the Fireside, I*
    WBT
    12-27-48 P.M.
    first 16:07 minutes

Swannee	Family/Larry
A Pretty Girl	Family/Danny
Tea for Two	Pat/Larry
What Are You Doing New Year's Eve?	Betty
Instrumental	Larry/Clarence/Arthur

26–B. *Fun by the Fireside, I* (inside out) WBT 12-27-48 P.M. last 12:30 minutes		
	Moonlight and Roses	Pat/Danny
	When You Wish Upon a Star	Pat
	Starlight, Star Bright	Family/Larry
	You Are My Lucky Star	Family/Larry
	I Told Every Little Star	Betty
	When You Wish Upon a Star	Family/Larry
	A Star Fell Out of Heaven	Danny
	You're the Only Star in My Blue Heaven	Family/Larry
	I Saw Stars	Larry
	Starlight, Star Bright	Family/Larry
	The Star Will Remember	Pat
	When You Wish Upon a Star	Danny
	Stardust	Family/Larry
	When You Wish Upon a Star	Family/Larry

27. *Quaker Oats* (inside out) (Announcer: Grady Cole) CBS No. 30 14:30 minutes		
	I Feel Like Shouting	Family/Larry
	Little Eyes, I Love You	Pa/Boys
	Farther Along	Family/Larry
	Have I Told You Lately That I Loved You?	Betty/Red
	On Moonlight Bay	Family/Larry

28. *Quaker Oats* (inside out) CBS No. 35 13:56 minutes		
	He Is Calling	Family/Larry
	Telling My Troubles to My Old Guitar	Family/Larry
	Have You Ever Been Lonely?	Betty
	When It's Lamplighting Time in the Valley	Pa/Boys
	In the Land of the Unsetting Sun	Family/Larry

29. *Quaker Oats* CBS No. 37 13:55 minutes		
	I Know I Have Religion	Family/Larry
	Polly Wolly Doodle	Pa/Boys
	Lead Me On	Family/Larry
	Candy and Cake	Betty
	Did You Ever Go Sailing?	Family/Larry

30. *Quaker Oats* (inside out) CBS No. 42 14:00 minutes		
	There Are Smiles	Family/Larry
	Billie Boy	Betty/Red
	I'd Like to Feel at Home	Family/Larry
	Boots and Saddles	Betty/Boys
	What Kind of Church Would My Church Be	Family/Larry

31. *Quaker Oats*	In Paradise Valley	Family/Larry
CBS	Up a Lazy River	Family/Betty
No. 66, June 1951	You've Gotta Walk That Long,	
14 minutes	Lonesome Road	Family/Larry
	I'm Throwing Rice	Pa/Boys
	Dear Ole Daddy	Family/Larry
32. *Quaker Oats*	The Stars and Stripes Forever	Family/Larry
CBS	When the Zephyrs of Heaven Shall	
No. 68, June 1951	Fan Me to Sleep	Family/Larry
13:52 minutes	Dig a Little Deeper	Family/Larry
	Deliverance Will Come	Family/Larry
	Sing, Neighbor, Sing!	Family/Larry
33. *Saturday Down South* (inside	When You Wore a Tulip	Family/Larry
out)	Pretty Kitty Kelly	Family/Larry
(Announcer: Kurt Webster)	Farther Along	Family/Larry
CBS	Sunday Morning in Dixie	Family/Larry
c.1947	There's a Goldmine in the Sky	Family/Larry
14:10 minutes		
34. *Saturday Down South* (inside	Apple-Blossom Time	Family/Larry
out)	Sentimental Journey	Family/Larry
CBS	Cabin in the Valley of the Pines	Family/Larry
c.1947	The Old Rugged Cross	Family/Larry
14:15 minutes	Swing Wide Yo' Golden Gates	Family/Larry
35. *The Song's for You* (inside	If I Could Be With You	Chris
out)	I'm in the Mood for Love	Betty
WBT	Maybe It's Because	Betty/Chris
09-11-49, 12:05 P.M.	Stars in My Eyes	Clarence
36. *The Song's for You* (inside	Where Are You?	Betty
out)	There Must Be a Way	Chris
WBT	You Came to Me From Out of	
12:05 P.M.	Nowhere	Clarence
	Love Is a Beautiful Thing	Betty/Chris
	I'm Confessing That I Love You	Betty
37. *Cut of Columbia Record*	I'll Reap My Harvest in Heaven	Family
20098		
04-01-46		
38. *Cut of Columbia Records*	Cabin in the Valley of the Pines	Family
20098 and 20369	Wait for the Light to Shine	Family
04-01-46		

39. *Margaret Ann Show*   Sweet and Lovely   Larry
    (Announcer: Larry Walker)   The Day After Forever   Pat
    Regional   Sweet and Lovely   Instrumental
    11-29-44   Look for the Silver Lining   Larry/Pat
                                          If That's the Way You Want It   Larry

40. *Margaret Ann Show*   I'm Looking Over a Four-Leaf Clover   Larry
    Regional   A Prayer (J. B. Clark)   Pat
    11-30-44   You've Got to Walk That Long,
                                             Lonesome Road   Family/Larry
                                          The White Cliffs of Dover   Pat
                                          I'm Just a Stowaway   Family/Pat/Larry

INDEX

Taylor, "Goat" and Cora, 69
Taylor, "Mutt," 19
Tennessee, 40
Tennessee Plowboy, The, 78
Tennessee Ramblers, 63
Tennessee River, 41
Terrell, TX, 29, 42
Texas, 33, 42
Thacker's Dairy, 10
"There's a Little Pine Log Cabin," 33, 34, 64
There's Music in the Air, 81
Thurmond, Senator Strom, 73
Tickle, Jim, 34
"Tie Me to Your Apron Strings Again," 96–97
Time, 83
Tobacco farming, 12, 36
Tonight Show, The, 82, 83
Tornado, 27, 28
Trailer, 41
Tredwell, Ken, 72
Triangle, NC, 43, 44
"Tribute to Dad, A," 95
Trinity Church, 43
Trinity Music, 77, 82
Troy, NY, 51
Tubb, Ernest, 73
Tunney, Gene, 54
Two Sisters' Farm, 85

"Uncle Andy," 46
Union, SC, 73, 77
University of New Hampshire, 86
USO program, 65

VA hospitals, 65
Vagabonds, 30, 47
Vale, NC, 40
Vaughan, James D., 32, 33, 45
Vaughan School of Music, 39
Veteran's Hospital Programs, 79, 80
Vick Chemical Co., 56
Victor Baptist Church, 61
Victor Grammar School, 61
Virginia Polytechnic Institute, 81
Volvo, 85

WAYS (Charlotte, NC), 69

WBIG (Greensboro, NC), 37
WBT (Charlotte, NC), 30, 40, 43, 45, 46–49, 53–56, 63, 72, 95
WBTV (Charlotte, NC), 50, 79
WDIX (Orangeburg, SC), 87, 95
WGST (Atlanta, GA), 55
WOAN (Lawrenceburg, TN), 38
WRVA (Richmond, VA), 55
WSM (Nashville, TN), 38
WSOC-TV (Charlotte, NC), 50
WSPA (Spartanburg, SC), 62
WTOP (Washington, DC), 67
"Wait for the Light to Shine," 69
"Wait 'til the Sun Shines, Nellie," 63
Walker, Dr. Laurens, 51
Walker, Larry (Laurens Bradham), 32, 48–50, 52, 53, 56, 57, 62, 71, 72, 91; Pat Walker, 50, 51, 53, 88
Wallace Fowler Publications, 70, 71
War Bonds, 65
Warm Springs, GA, 65
Warren, Elmer ("Hank"), 56, 63
Washington, DC, 83; Gallaudet College, 51
Washington, President George, 85
Watermelon patch, 36
Watson, Frank, 97
Webster, Kurt, 49, 58
Weems, Ted, 58
Welch, Clarence ("Cat"), 13
Wesley, John, 28, 62
West, Dottie, 78
Westford Methodist Church, 61
Westminster Choir College, 66
Wheeling, WV, 80
"When the Family Gets Together Round the Old Log Cabin," 72
"When You Wore a Tulip," 52
"Where No Cabins Fall," 64
"Where We'll Never Grow Old," 59
"Whispering Hope," 82
White, Don, 56, 63
White, Nannie, 27
White Oak Transfer Co., 22
White Sulphur Springs, WV, 60
Whitey and Hogan, 56, 63
Willard, Jess (boxer), 50